'Our secular Western age assumes that life's primary purpose is to feel good. Here we are reminded that the Christian's purpose for living is not to feel good but, by God's grace, to become good, to be godly. And Christ-likeness only occurs when we take up our cross and follow him. This is more than a primer for graduating students seeking to count the cost for overseas missions. It's a book that reminds all Christians of the cost and high privilege of true discipleship. I recommend it highly!'

Rebecca Manley Pippert
Salt Shaker Ministries

'Here is the antidote to the deadly lie that getting my own way is what is best for me. Here is God's call to liberating, costly obedience, even unto death, in the full knowledge that Jesus is with us even unto death. *Jesus says 'Go!'* is an honest, compassionate and uncompromisingly biblical examination of the struggle to say "no" to self and "yes" to God.'

Don Cormack
Author of *Killing Fields, Living Fields*

'There is an urgent need to heed the message of this book. It convincingly presents key biblical emphases which have been neglected by the Church, influenced as it is by the culture of our day. I believe that churches in affluent countries which neglect it stand the risk of disqualifying themselves from being missionary-sending churches.'

Ajith Fernando
Sri Lanka Youth for Christ

'We only have one life to live. Taking the gospel to the world is one of the best ways we can invest it for God. This book highlights the joys, as well as the cost, of overseas mission, be it long or short-term. We need to absorb this book, act on it and give it to our friends.'
Rachel Green
Interserve On-Track

'We've let compromise and a low commitment to self-denial keep us sidelined for too long. This book is a great resource for those who are ready to turn their back on these hindrances and join the company God is raising up in this pivotal hour – radicals who will do whatever it takes to bring the message of Jesus to the nations. Don't just read it, but pray through it, committing yourself afresh to living it!'
Ryan Shaw
Student Volunteer Movement 2

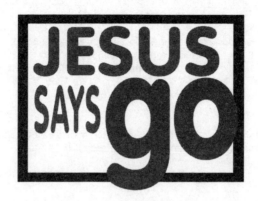

Robin Wells

Foreword by George Verwer

MONARCH
B O O K S

Oxford, UK & Grand Rapids, Michigan, USA

In partnership with

First published in the UK in 2006 by Monarch Books
(a publishing imprint of Lion Hudson plc),
Mayfield House, 256 Banbury Road, Oxford OX2 7DH
Tel: +44 (0) 1865 302750   Fax: +44 (0) 1865 302757
Email: monarch@lionhudson.com
www.lionhudson.com

Published in conjunction with the International Fellowship of
Students (IFES), SIM and OMF

An earlier version of this book was published in 2000 as *My Rights,
My God*

Distributed by:
UK: Marston Book Services Ltd, PO Box 269,
Abingdon, Oxon OX14 4YN;
USA: Kregel Publications, PO Box 2607,
Grand Rapids, Michigan 49501.

ISBN-13: 978-1-85424-730-8 (UK)
ISBN-10: 1-85424-730-1 (UK)
ISBN-13: 978-0-8254-6114-9 (USA)
ISBN-10: 0-8254-6114-6 (USA)

British Library Cataloguing Data
A catalogue record for this book is available from
the British Library.

Printed in Great Britain.

About the author

Robin Wells is South African. He studied
Chemistry at the University of Pretoria,
and then gained his doctorate from
Imperial College, London. Robin has been active in student
ministry in South Africa, and more widely as a member of
the Executive Committee of the International Fellowship of
Evangelical Students (IFES); he served as General Secretary
of the Universities and Colleges Christian Fellowship
(UCCF), its UK movement, for twelve years. More recently
his work with the Africa Evangelical Fellowship, which
became part of SIM, included help with the selection and
training of missionaries.

For Val

Contents

INTERLUDE

PART II

THE LAST WORD

Acknowledgments

First I must thank everyone whose kind comments about this book have spurred me on. I am grateful to Rose Dowsett for contributing Part II. Mission is in the character of God, so our calling is from him.

The idea for this revised and expanded edition of my former book came from Julia Cameron of IFES. My thanks go to her as critical and encouraging editor. I am also grateful to Tony Collins, Director of Monarch Books, for his contribution to its shaping and development. Various conversations along the way and comments from a range of people have, I hope, helped to make the text widely useful. I am particularly grateful to Scott Bessenecker and Becky Stephen of InterVarsity USA; Navin Singh of InterVarsity Canada; Mark Grace of TSCF New Zealand; Iván Neira of OM; Richard Tiplady of ECM; Jonathan Edwards of YWAM; Yvonne Choo of FES Singapore; Michael Raiter of the Bible College of Victoria; Howard Spencer of AFES Australia; Rosanne Jones of OMF International; John Williams of UCCF UK; Sam Allberry of St Ebbe's Church, Oxford; Paul Lindsay of Christian Vocations; Martin Lee of Global Connections; and my daughter Bethan Parmenter.

A special word of thanks goes to my wife Val for her forbearance and encouragement, not only in the writing of this book, but in our ministry over the years. Thanks, too, to my AEF/SIM and UCCF friends and colleagues who shared in all the pains and joys of involvement in mission.

RJW

Robin Wells has a track record as one of God's marathon runners. I hope that many potential runners for the Kingdom will let these pages help them get into the race and stay in it.

This unique and important book is especially needed today when everyone is bombarded with postmodern culture. It is hardly surprising that people grow up to distrust authority and to celebrate autonomy. Our easy lifestyles and high disposable incomes make it all the harder to keep gospel priorities at the front of our thinking. Robin's analysis of the 'cultures of comfort' needs to be taken to heart. I believe *Jesus says 'Go!'* helps us find a glorious and biblical path through the confusion and darkness of the Western mindset.

This powerful message on the Lordship of Christ should impact every aspect of our lives. In short, here is a well thoughtout and compelling presentation. Let's not ignore it. It is especially relevant to those who want to spend their lives in cross-cultural ministry, but it is more than that. It is a valuable and needed message for every one of us.

It is my prayer that people will not only read and study this book, but will take it seriously enough to play a part in getting it out to others – not only in their own country, but across the globe. I long for God's people to realise afresh the power of the printed page, and to become more committed in their reading and distribution of books like this.

George Verwer
Founder and first International Director,
Operation Mobilisation

PART I

JESUS SAYS 'GO!'

Jesus said: 'All authority in heaven and on earth has been given to me. Therefore go and make disciples of all nations, baptising them in the name of the Father and of the Son and of the Holy Spirit, and teaching them to obey everything I have commanded you. I am with you always, to the very end of the age.' (Matthew 28:18–20)

This book has something for everyone. Yet it is written especially for those who still have most of their lives ahead of them, and who may be facing big decisions about their futures – possibly including long-term mission. Though some of it was written with long-term mission in mind, most of the issues we touch on will be basic biblical truths, relevant to short-termers as well as to long-termers, part of the fibre of the Christian life.

I pray particularly that those serving short-term will find

the early chapters helpful, and will make time to engage
with some of the questions raised in the chapters further
on before they travel.

So you are exploring a possible call from God to serve
him in another culture? You will need to face the
implications of what that will mean. If that is where you
are, perhaps you already realise that such a call can be
costly. You may have friends who have taken that path,
and you may have seen something of what it has meant
for them – financial or career sacrifices, separation from
family and friends, and so on.

Jason writes of how he came to explore these matters.
With 19,000 others at the Urbana Missions Convention,
he heard how God could use him to help pioneer an
evangelical student movement in the Muslim world. In
discussion with his pastor and older Christian friends,
Jason looked at the necessary sacrifices. There were hard
questions. He had a degree in Business and Economics
and had just secured a job in investment banking. 'Am I
willing to give up my career? Can I bear not seeing my
family for two years? Can I say goodbye to my girlfriend?'
Over the next year he saw his father's opposition change
to enthusiastic support. The funding he needed came in.
As this book is published he is living under a Muslim
government as part of a small team. Through offering
friendship and English teaching, he and the others are
slowly winning the confidence of students. Progress will
take prayer and perseverance, but their sights are set.
With God's help they will establish an IFES movement to
bring the gospel of Christ to that country's students.

The purpose of this book is to explore all these kinds of
costs, and their compensations, and to look at them in the
light of the Bible.

We need to be realistic. Jesus doesn't call us to act

impulsively or unthinkingly. We should carefully count the cost of Christian discipleship, whatever the path we take. We are to look at the pros and cons with open eyes. There are big issues at stake. There are real costs, but also substantial benefits! If we are serious about following Christ, there can be no doubt about the bottom line: putting him first always gives the best outcome.

These issues raise serious questions for those who live in the West or in countries with comparable standards of living: people from the 'cultures of comfort'. In the ease and affluence of our lives, making sacrifices can seem unreasonable. The world we live in whispers in our ears that we are entitled to hold on to every comfort – that we have a right to do so. Christians, like everyone else, breathe in this atmosphere and need to be aware that this is happening. We cannot be immune to the influences around us. So we need always to be letting the Bible interrogate our world, and also our own personal patterns of belief and behaviour.

Protecting our rights has been a strong theme in the Western world through the past three or four generations. We see it emerge in all sorts of ways: in political conflicts; in debates on gender issues; in questions thrown up by medical progress. But how godly a theme is it? Any one of these areas can create a mindset that jealously protects our 'rights' against God's authority, and shields us against any calling to make sacrifices; a mindset that challenges Christ's lordship in our lives.

So why should you follow a costly path – if that's the way God is calling you? What right have I to encourage you in that? Well, I have no right, but I have a responsibility. You and I stand together under the authority of the Bible, and of the Lord of whom the Bible speaks. And that brings on us a responsibility to help each other in our discipleship and in our obedience to the Scriptures.

This Lord of whom the Bible speaks is the Lord Jesus whose cross is at the centre of our faith. I was struck recently by this remark: 'We will take sacrifice seriously only if we understand the cross.' When Jesus taught his disciples that he would have to die on the cross, he gave them the cross as a pattern for their discipleship. (See, for example, Mark 8:31–38.) Christians, then, bear the imprint of the cross on their lives. So we should not be surprised if the Christian life calls for some toughness: he told us it would.

> **Christians bear the imprint of the cross on their lives.**

Now let's turn to the last meal Jesus had with his inner circle of friends before his death. He taught them that, in his death, his body was being given for them. 'This is my body,' he said, 'given for you.' So as we take part in the Lord's Supper or Communion service, we are helped to see ourselves, as individuals, needing his death for us. 'He loved me and gave himself for me,' said Paul (Galatians 2:20).

But in the accounts of both Matthew and Mark, we have a second emphasis alongside that. Jesus gives his disciples the shared cup of wine with these words: 'This is my blood of the covenant, which is poured out for many' (Matthew 26:28; Mark 14:24). Not only for them, but 'for many'. In the intense privacy of that upper room he directs their thoughts outwards, to the waiting world. They are to think not only of their own needs but also of the world into which he is sending them. Mission is of the essence of the gospel.

* * *

As we go through the book we'll meet a number of people who have already faced the questions of cost. We'll learn how they view them. I have talked to a wide range of people with experience of different continents. Many served first as short-termers while they were students. Most are still fairly young. There are things to be learned from those with greater experience, of course, and their stories come in too. In addition to these, some of the quotations I have used are 'classics'.

People have urged me, again and again, not to let realism about hardships overshadow the joys and satisfaction of serving God in costly paths. Talk of the 'joy of sacrifice', they said. And I note that they are people who have been through a good deal of suffering in their own lives.

If, when you have finished this book, you really want to do business with God over your future, do it. Don't let the attractions of the career package – or anything else – crowd out what God may be saying to you. To help you in this, read some good missionary biography: you could start with an account of

> **If you really want to do business with God over your future, do it.**

one of the great missionary pioneers like Hudson Taylor, William Carey, David Brainerd, Adoniram Judson, Sadhu Sundar Singh or John Sung. But read contemporary stories of the Church too. These will all help you build a fuller picture of world mission, and give you insights into what people have endured for the sake of the gospel. Ask your church leaders, or missionaries you know, for recommendations. I have included websites you can browse. Those of us who have worked on putting this book together will be praying that God would be at work in the lives of its readers. Whatever you do with your future, may it bring him glory.

CHAPTER 1

Cultures of comfort

There is a wonderful honesty and realism in the Bible. It offers us no escapism. It doesn't try to trick us into any action by hiding the consequences from us. Jesus himself warns us that the Christian life is costly: following him is no easy option. In fact, Jesus explicitly calls us to take stock of our lives and weigh up the cost of discipleship. He tells us that anyone who wants to be his disciple 'must deny himself and

> **The Bible offers us no escapism.**

take up his cross'. This is his baseline for serious-minded discipleship, and so we open our first chapter with by reminding ourselves of that.

All discipleship is costly. But some people are called to a costlier path than others, and serving overseas can be one example of this. It is a myth, by the way, that a tough and sacrificial lifestyle is easier for missionaries than it would be for others, just because God has called them to it. They are made no differently from us and feel suffering as much. The pain is as real for them as it would be for anybody.

So why should anyone take that path? Why should we

give up the prospect of a decent house, a nice car, a good salary, and a benefits package that will see us into an early retirement full of good holidays? Why not stay in our own country and make a name for ourselves in our profession?

After all, no role is wrong in itself. We can please God in any legitimate occupation. There is no sense in which it is a 'more spiritual' calling to work overseas, and there are situations in our own country where it can be very tough to be a Christian. And the voice saying these things in our ears, distracting us from our high calling, is reinforced by the world we live in.

> **There are situations in our own country where it can be very tough to be a Christian.**

Amusing ourselves to death

We in the West live in a very comfortable world. And we keep on expecting ever more comfort and convenience. We can usually find quick relief from pain when we are ill or have an accident. Many previously life-threatening conditions are now almost trivial, thanks to medical advances. Just think back to what life was like for our great-grandparents before the discovery of anaesthetics or even antibiotics. How different our world is from theirs!

The wealthy and inventive cultures in the West have produced any number of ways for us to amuse and entertain ourselves, and it is no longer just the rich who can afford them. That is the case whether we like going on energetic skiing holidays or prefer to settle for the physically less demanding option of computer games. No surprise, then, that Neil Postman, Professor of Communication Arts and Sciences at New York University, should entitle his reflection on our culture *Amusing Ourselves to Death*.

The 20th-century Christian philosopher Francis Schaeffer coined the term 'personal peace and affluence' to describe what drives human aspirations in the postmodern world. This was most perceptive. Without conscious thought, we drift towards that, and away from service which is costly. Let's recognise this bias in ourselves, and be aware of the dangers. It stems from a self-fulfilling and self-indulgent mindset, in which the aim is far removed from pleasing God.

We are living in a world which has anaesthetised itself to horror and tragedy. We can still say 'What a pity, those poor people', but our emotions are left intact. The upbeat music at the end of the news bulletin has pulled us back into what we are beguiled into thinking is 'reality'. We enjoy the comfort of an armchair thousands of miles from the area of conflict, the drought, or the plane crash. We might as well have been hearing news of another world, another planet. Our own comfort zone has not been invaded, and we have looked on as voyeurs, entertained by the plight of fellow human beings for whom Christ died.

> **We look on as voyeurs, entertained by the plight of fellow human beings for whom Christ died.**

If we look at things in the sweep of human history, we should note that our prosperous and comfortable world is most unusual. No one in any culture or with whatever riches has ever lived as comfortably as we do now. The comparative freedom from wars that impinge on us and on our families and friends is also an unusual blip in history. We have grown up in a war-free comfort zone, and have come to take it for granted. We assume it is the norm. Yes, there are conflicts, famines, floods, droughts and other natural disasters in far-off places. But these are all mediated through television reports, news websites or print media. They do not really touch our lives.

In no way is the West of the last few generations typical of human history. If we build our lives and our views of the world on the belief that it is, we are building on sand. If we assume we have the right to such a lifestyle we fly in the face of world realities. History also shows us that no one – not even the privileged few – can entirely escape pain or disappointment. These things are part of the human predicament. In spite of all that has been opened up to us through our education, and through medical and technological progress, we know frustration, pain and death, and there is nothing we can do to avoid them. What's wrong? Why, when we are created with desires and the capacity for pleasure, is there this sense of futility in the world?

This is a key question. And as with so many issues which touch on what it means to be human, we find ourselves needing to look back to the story of creation to explore it. Can we find a framework that makes sense of our desires for pleasure and also makes sense of the need at times to say 'No' to legitimate aspirations?

Where it all went wrong

We need to start the story where the story starts, with God's creation of a world that he described as 'very good'. We can't understand exactly what that 'very good' world was like, but it is clear that it was very different from the world we live in. It, and all beings in it, perfectly fulfilled the roles they were created for, and reflected the glory of

God. What a world! Then swiftly the scene changes, and in Genesis 3 the Bible turns our attention to a darker picture.

The first man and woman, created with a capacity for pleasure but also accountable to their Creator, are seduced into an act of rebellion which theologians call 'the Fall'. It was to leave the whole human race with many scars.

Were it not for this event in our history, this book would not be written. There would be no need for Christian witness, for the whole world would be in fellowship with God as Creator. There is a sense in which all of human experience finds Genesis 3 as its reference point. For a true understanding of what it is to be human and of why we need salvation, it is the key.

> **There is a sense in which all of human experience finds Genesis 3 as its reference point.**

One outcome of 'the Fall' is that we always seem dissatisfied. We end up hoping for things that cannot fulfil their promise. Another result is that our desire for what is good becomes distorted: the things we long for do not reflect a longing for perfect harmony between child and heavenly Father, but instead express defiance and resentment. We desire what we want, and we no longer desire only what he wants. The rebellion recounted in Genesis 3 aimed to place us on the throne that is rightfully God's. As a result of this, we are born as fallen human beings, and with a mistaken sense that it is our 'right' to satisfy our desires.

This is universal, of course, but it is particularly noticeable in the West. We believe we have rights to unlimited comfort and safety, and we look for someone to blame when things go wrong.

25

There are good and legitimate uses of the word 'rights', but more often than not it is used in defiance of authority, and particularly of God's authority. When through Adam's sin we became rebels, we all fell under God's judgment and we all forfeited our rights. The language of 'rights' can become the language of rebellion against God. It often is just that.

What of the Christian? Do we share in the futility that grips the human race? The answer is both yes and no. God's plan of redemption is full and perfect. We have a certain hope of a new creation – including us – that will be perfect in every respect, free from all disappointment and discomfort. But that is in the future. We can't expect full satisfaction now. In the meantime we share in the pains and imperfections of life, but with a perspective that transforms it all.

Getting things in perspective

As I have talked with the people whose stories are in this book, I have been repeatedly struck by one thing. They show no self-pity, nor any regret for having obeyed Christ. Why is this? I sat at a meal in Cochabamba, Bolivia, with a number of SIM missionaries, and we talked around these things. 'The issue is perspective,' said one American missionary.

The issue is perspective.

There is a great biblical principle in that. We see the principle in the examples of Jesus himself and the Apostle Paul. They didn't look at their sufferings in isolation. They put them in perspective alongside other things; they made comparisons. Listen to how it is put in the letter to the Hebrews: 'Let us fix our eyes on Jesus … who for the joy set before him endured the cross, scorning its shame'

(Hebrews 12:2). He put the suffering of the cross alongside the miracle of all that the cross would accomplish, and doing this enabled him to 'scorn' its pain.

Paul, too, suffered for his faith, and like his master he was able to put it in perspective. At the end of a passage in which he gives an appalling description of his sufferings, he writes: 'Our light and momentary troubles are achieving for us an eternal glory that far outweighs them all. So we fix our eyes not on what is seen, but on what is unseen. For what is seen is temporary, but what is unseen is eternal' (2 Corinthians 4:17,18). Paul didn't deny the reality of his sufferings, but he was able to see them as 'light and momentary' in comparison with unseen but eternal realities.

A recent example: I was talking to a young missionary whose experiences are recounted in these chapters. He and his wife and children were living in the Philippines, in a tough situation. I asked him what had kept them there when the going got tough. No doubt with the parable of the talents in mind (see Matthew 25:14–23), he responded, 'I didn't want to miss the "Well done".' He had the perspective!

'I didn't want to miss the "Well done."'

This view of hardships makes sense of the passages in the New Testament that call us to rejoice in sufferings. It is no perverted masochism, enjoying pain for its own sake. It is a triumph of perspective. Take Jesus' own words to his followers: 'Blessed are you when people insult you, persecute you and falsely say all kinds of evil against you because of me. Rejoice and be glad, because great is your reward in heaven' (Matthew 5:11,12).

So Paul writes, 'We rejoice in our sufferings' (Romans

5:3); he can do this because of the results he sees flowing into people's lives through those sufferings. He goes on: 'suffering produces perseverance, perseverance character, and character hope.' In turn, James urges: 'Consider it pure joy, my brothers, whenever you face trials of many kinds' (James 1:2). His reasons? 'The testing of your faith develops perseverance. Perseverance must finish its work so that you may be mature and complete, not lacking anything.'

A final example of perspective, this time from C T Studd, the famous 19th century sportsman and missionary: 'If Jesus Christ be God and died for me, there can be no sacrifice too great for me to make for him.'

Getting real

These are not examples of mindless fanaticism. They are calls to use our minds and make serious comparisons. This book is a serious call to look at the 'bottom line'. Is the 'bottom line' to be seen entirely in financial terms, and in the benefits money can buy us and our families? A mortgage paid off in time for early retirement? A good school for our children?

> **This book is a serious call to look at the 'bottom line'.**

If we know our God, and we want to make it our aim to please him, our horizons will be further away. We will look to things that are unseen. For some of us there will be a comfortable lifestyle, but we shall hold it lightly, and as a trust from God. For others of us, we shall be finding out what Christ meant by the 'hundred times' return he promised to those who give up homes and families for his sake (see Matthew 19:29).

you may be starting to understand how complex 'culture' is.

Retreating like that may be OK if we don't need to relate to the local people in any meaningful way. But if they are really the whole reason why we're there, we need to find a better solution.

Kevin and Liz Wren's story

Kevin and Liz Wren have been serving with OMF in the UK, co-ordinating the Fellowship's short-termers. When I first met them they were rookie missionaries in the Philippines. Kevin described their situation then very poetically as 'living on the beach'. As you read that story, you'll get a better feel for the reality:

Living on the beach may sound romantic, but perhaps we should rephrase it to living beside the rubbish tip, as that's the nearest thing we could really compare it to. It wasn't luxury, but we'd never been so happy and excited as we felt then.

Our neighbours were down-to-earth, fun-loving people, despite their extreme poverty. They had time on their hands, so they always wanted to chat with us. This made us feel at home and was great for our language practice. They were also generous, always giving us fish that they'd caught. And they took Kevin fishing too.

As our homes were so close, we were with them from morning till night. Our house was newly-built and made of concrete, with two rooms upstairs and one downstairs, plus a shower/toilet. The fishermen's bamboo huts had neither shower nor toilet. They washed under the water pump outside our kitchen window, and used the beach and the sea as a toilet. In the mornings we heard them going out to fish, any time from 3 a.m. onwards.

Life could be hard and stressful, and we tired easily and needed to keep our spiritual lives in good shape. But we loved the wonderful chance to get into the local language, and the friendly atmosphere in which to witness. The first time that I (Liz) saw my nearest neighbour, I was frightened of her. She was well-built, and her decibel level would have made anyone jump. A couple of days later I was woken in the night by her youngest child crying. I was frightened to go and see what was wrong, but felt I had to. The little boy was sick, so I gave her some Calpol for him. At 4.30 a.m. I heard excited voices outside telling the story of how the 'foreign' woman had come to help.

> **We needed to keep our spiritual lives in good shape.**

After this, we became friends. They started to visit us often, to chat, cook, eat, and look at our photographs. The local children started to come, too, to play with Jonathan and Matthew and with their toys.

We wrote to our prayer partners and asked them to give thanks with us for our home and our new friends. And we urged them to pray that God would move by his Spirit so the fishermen in Lemery [Philippines] would choose to follow him, just as Peter and Andrew had in Galilee.

Greg and Kelly Johnson's story

Greg and Kelly Johnson live in Central Asia. They come from South Africa where Greg worked as a Project Manager in the High Voltage industry, and Kelly as a legal secretary for a Labour attorney. Greg is managing a project to help poor families start up small businesses such as drying tomatoes, raising bulls and selling them for profit. Kelly has been running a beginners' English course at the centre for children, and now teaches Life Skills to the community's youth. She writes:

I don't think we realised just how different a culture we were coming to live in. Sure, we knew there were differences, but we never imagined their vastness and depth.

At first it was fun. We discovered simple things like taking and receiving with our right hands, praying with our hands cupped in front of us, and removing our shoes before entering a home. These were relatively easy to adapt to. Shopping at the food bazaar was a novelty and using the archaic transport system an adventure. In this country it is an offence to wear a seatbelt, as the government feels it is safer not to! And you can get fined for driving a dirty car!

There were so many national food dishes that we got to taste, spices we'd never smelt and fruits we'd never seen before. It was a learning experience that drew on every one of our senses. And the people – we were bowled over by their warmth. Were they abnormally friendly, or had we come from a society that had grown cold and unfriendly?

But after being here a few months, reality started to sink in. We were not on an extended vacation and this strange, often confusing culture was one we needed to learn to live with, and even love. Things we had at first thought 'cute' became irritating. Our host family persistently told us to *take, take* at meal times. At first we found this caring, but then we started to view it as annoying, and an attempt to make us overeat.

> **Things we had at first thought 'cute' became irritating.**

The part we have found hardest has been the differences in crucial values. I guess we expected that at the core of all cultures, crucial values would be the same or very similar. An incident with our neighbour taught us otherwise. Through this incident we learnt that saving face and loyalty to family are held in higher regard than truth and honesty. That was a bitter pill for us to swallow.

Culture is more complex than you think

Why is this process of entering another culture such a battle? First, because culture is so much more complicated than we realise, and also because our own culture is 'transparent' to us. We are like a goldfish in a bowl. He can look through the glass and see the outside world, but he can't see the water that is his own world. Our culture is drip-fed into us from our earliest months, and we live it

> **We unconsciously assume that all humans function as we do.**

unconsciously. We don't think of ourselves as practising our culture: we simply are what we are! And we unconsciously assume that all humans function as we do.

What is culture? One definition goes like this: Culture is all learned behaviour which is socially acquired, that is, the material and non-material traits which are passed on from one generation to another. Thus the ability to eat is instinctive, not learned, and is not part of culture. But different ways of eating – knife and fork, chopsticks, fingers – are learned: they are part of 'culture'. The ability to sing is not 'culture', but using twelve tones to the octave, or five, is socially acquired, and is 'culture'.

Another example. We all use our hands to pass things to someone else, or to receive things from them. That is what hands are designed for, and isn't culture. But some people-groups teach their children from their earliest years, as Kelly and Greg discovered, that it is proper to use only the right hand for this, never the left. They use the left hand only for personal hygiene, and it is 'unclean' for other uses. Children grow up instinctively and quite unconsciously using their hands in these ways. To be forced to use the left hand for anything other than personal hygiene would be awkward, offensive, embarrassing! That is part of their culture.

> **To use the left hand would be offensive, embarrassing!**

The same principles arise in all sorts of behaviour patterns: how we ask questions, how groups come to collective decisions, how the genders and the generations treat each other, and so on. And just as we may be unconscious of our own cultural distinctive, many in our host country will be unconscious of theirs. We may find we relate to them with minimal trouble, even without our or their being very conscious of the cultural gulf – until the moment we say or do something that is completely natural to us, but that is unnatural, and perhaps offensive, to them.

I remember watching a group of young people in an African town. There were perhaps eight of them, including two Westerners. At first, they were chatting freely and happily among themselves, but then I noticed that the African members of the group had gone silent. The Westerners carried on, oblivious to the change. Clearly they had said something, in all ignorance, that cut across the African cultural norms. (As I recall, the difference was in the area of how generations relate to one another.) I sensed the Africans were mystified, rather than offended, by the Westerners' different underlying assumptions.

I sensed the Africans were mystified, rather than offended.

Of course, the offence can be the other way round. A young missionary couple are working in a village in the Philippines. They live in a house that opens straight onto the street. Some of their windows, likewise, open onto the street. They describe how difficult they found it when the villagers, in a way quite natural to them, would spend perhaps half an hour standing outside the windows, peering in! In the West we guard our privacy quite jealously. We close our front

In the West we guard our privacy quite jealously.

36

doors and draw our curtains when it gets dark. We're home. We can choose whether to answer the doorbell, or the phone. We can choose whether to check email or have an evening without any intrusion whatsoever: human, voice or electronic. We are in charge. But this young couple cannot do that. They have chosen to forgo what Westerners consider their inalienable right. It can be hard not to resent people behaving in ways that intrude on us, or cause us inconvenience and even offence. But that may be a price we are called to pay.

Getting to the point where we can live effectively in another culture, and have relationships beyond the superficial, takes time and effort, as we see from the Johnsons' story. It's not easy, and it's not always pleasant or comfortable. I was struck by the way Kevin and Liz Wren had handled this in their first term in the Philippines, when they were just out of language school. They believed the Lord wanted them to live in a particular town, but there wasn't anywhere available to rent. So they settled for the house among fishermen on the beach. It was no picnic, as you'll have seen from their story. But the Wrens are no ordinary couple. Kevin left school at seventeen and became an itinerant evangelist. He learned the art of fire-eating, which could often draw a crowd! Liz trained as a nurse.

> **He learned the art of fire-eating, which could often draw a crowd!**

After they had been married a short time, both sensed God's call on their lives, and they started to explore the possibility of working in Asia. It would be a wrench to leave families and friends behind, and Liz felt that keenly. But as they talked and prayed about it they found

37

themselves echoing the apostle Paul's words: 'Christ's love compels us' (2 Corinthians 5:14). They later moved elsewhere in East Asia, to an area where their neighbours were all Muslims – another new culture, more trust to build, more friendships to build. Since then they have been back in the UK, working to recruit and equip short-termers, and to help them see their time in Asia as a prelude to a lifetime of mission service. That is a wonderful goal for *all* short-termers, whether they return to their host culture in a long-term role, or remain in their home culture and actively encourage others in their church to pray for and support world mission.

Do I need to change?

This is a good question. Learning to live in our host culture won't be easy. At times it will feel like a denial of our very identity. Why should I put up with that inconvenience? Haven't I the right just to be myself? If that's how God has shaped me, can't I stay that way?

The issue is underlined when we see how far some people go in maintaining an environment that reflects their home culture. Their homes, even their cars, are little enclaves of America or Europe.

> **Their homes, even their cars, are little enclaves of America or Europe.**

Of course, there is a limit to the extent we can or need to 'become like them'. No matter how long you live in your host culture, and no matter what efforts you make to conform to it, you can never become fully one of them. It's just not possible. Even where you come to behave as they do, it will often be behaviour that you have consciously learned and may still exercise consciously. They have acquired it unconsciously and exercise it unconsciously, as we all do in our own culture. We may well adopt some parts of their behaviour unconsciously, but other things – even when we get it almost right – will always be done consciously. So it is futile to hope to be able to become completely like them.

Neither would they expect us to become completely like them. We may reach a stage when we are so comfortable in our host culture that we feel quite inconspicuous. Yet our friends from the host culture will always be aware of our foreignness, and they accept that as part of us. They take it for granted; it is not resented. In fact, attempts to go too far can come across as strained, artificial, even patronising. They welcome the efforts we make to show respect to their culture and be able to relate well to them. They don't expect us to become one of them.

> **Our friends will always be aware of our foreignness, and accept that as part of us.**

Well then, do you have to change? If you have any thoughts of serving the people in your host country, then surely the answer has to be yes!

Look again at the person who strives to make every part of his environment as much like 'being back home' as he can. Make no mistake, his national friends will notice it. What signal does it give to them? It tells them that he would rather be home than in their country. Beyond that, it tells them that their Western friend is not only attached to his own culture (that would be accepted), but more, that he dislikes – even despises – theirs. They suspect that he thinks of his own culture as the truly Christian culture, superior in all respects to their own.

That view of our cultures is simply false! No culture deserves to be set up as the Christian culture: no culture ever has. Even if we can't see the blemishes in our own cultures, or the areas where our friends' culture is better,

> **No culture deserves to be set up as the Christian culture: no culture ever has.**

we may be sure they will. If, deep down, we believe our culture is superior to theirs, and betray that in our attitudes, we will certainly close their ears to what we might hope to tell them.

Think of some of the cultural features where there are differences between 'us' and 'them'. Take, for example, the ways of speaking that are seen as 'good manners'. Suppose that, after some time in our host country, we are still making the same mistakes we made in our early days, so that our friends wince as much at our apparent bad manners now as they did then. We'll simply appear rude to them. They will certainly find it impossible to believe that we love them. At best, their ears are likely to be closed to our message. At worst, they will avoid us or even treat us with hostility. Frankly, we will deserve it! If we are there to serve the King, the cost will include the pain and inconvenience of entering the world of our hosts.

What can we learn from Paul?

We can expect to find some light on this from the apostle Paul, the great missionary pioneer. Take, for example, the explanation he gives to the church in Corinth of some of his principles (1 Corinthians 9). Seven times in this chapter he uses the word 'right' or 'rights', and he claims certain rights. Then, in passionate language he sets out what matters more than these rights. His point in claiming them is to show that he is willing to give them up. In verse 19 he spells out the main principle:

> *Though I am free and belong to no man, I make myself a slave to everyone, to win as many as possible.*

Then he applies this to a range of issues – including cultural differences – that he faced in his ministry:

> *To the Jews I became like a Jew, to win the Jews. To those under the law I became like one under the law (though I myself am not under the law), so as to win those under the law. To those not having the law I became like one not having the law (though I am not free from God's law but am under Christ's law), so as to win those not having the law. To the weak I became weak, to win the weak.* (verses 20–22)

His principle was to adapt, where possible, to the cultures of those he aimed to reach. So in a final summarising statement he tells us:

> *I have become all things to all men so that by all possible*

*means I might save some. I
do all this for the sake of the
gospel, that I may share in its
blessings.* (verses 22,23)

For Paul, what was best for the gospel overshadowed his
'rights'.

A wise remark of John Calvin on a closely related
theme illustrates Paul's mind. Dealing with Christian
liberty, Calvin remarks that
Christian liberty is not lost, even if
it is never exercised.[1] Our
aggressive and self-assertive
world would tell us that the
essence of freedoms is to exercise
them, and the essence of rights is
to demand them. No, says Calvin,
reflecting the spirit shown here by
Paul. If, for the sake of others, I choose not to exercise my
freedom, I am in no way less free. So Paul writes, 'Though
I am free and belong to no man, I make myself a slave to
everyone, to win as many as
possible'. 'Though I *am* free', note,
not 'Though I *was* free'. The truly
free man or woman is free to
exercise a right or not to exercise
it! Either way, they remain free, if
they choose in this spirit of service
to others.

> **For Paul,
> what was best
> for the gospel
> overshadowed
> his 'rights'.**

> **Christian
> liberty is not
> lost, even if
> it is never
> exercised.**

Let's turn to a higher example –
that of the Lord Jesus Christ himself. We need to be
careful about drawing parallels between Christ's
experiences and ours: nothing that we might ever be

1. John Calvin, *Institutes of the Christian Religion*, Book III, Chapter 19

42

called on to endure can compare with his humiliation in becoming a man and dying for us. But we are encouraged in Scripture to look at him as an example for us in some things. Surely this is one.

In Philippians 2, Paul tells his readers to imitate Christ (see verse 5). In what way? In his willingness not to hold on to his 'right' to enjoy his status of equality with God. In this immeasurably costly identification with us, which Paul spells out for us step by breathtaking step, Christ goes down, not only to become man, but to die; not only to die, but to die a criminal's humiliating death (verses 6–8). He was called to do more than we could ever be called to. In Paul's terse phrase, 'he made himself nothing'.

Some other words of Paul's come to mind – good words to muse on as we close this chapter. Once more, Paul is using Christ as an example for us to follow:

> *You know the grace of our*
> *Lord Jesus Christ, that*
> *though he was rich, yet for*
> *your sakes he became poor,*
> *so that you through his*
> *poverty might become rich.*
> (2 Corinthians 8:9)

We have the gospel. We are rich. In a pale reflection of the Lord's ministry to us, will we 'become poor' to take this gospel to others?

CHAPTER 3

Expectations in our ministry

We live in an age when Christians are in danger of becoming preoccupied with finding 'fulfilment'. Is that to be found in exercising our gifts to the full? Even if it is, do we have a right to it? Should it be our goal? The 'me generation' seems to think so. There is, of course, a grain of truth here. The gifts God gives us are entrusted to us to use well. That, after all, is why we might be thinking of going abroad. We believe we have a message to bring, a contribution to make.

We enter our host country with a set of expectations about our potential usefulness. After all, it's surely not for nothing that God has called us to serve him there. And our gifts and experience at home have equipped us with something to bring to those we will live among. That's a sound way of thinking. In fact we should probably not be considering service overseas unless we have already shown in our home country that God has given us the gifts for it.

Beyond doubt, we work most effectively in activities that fit the gifts God has given us. And it can be a very rewarding experience. But God also calls

> **We work most effectively in activities that fit the gifts God has given us.**

us to think first of being useful to him and to others, and only second of our own fulfilment. It's rather like happiness in the Christian life. Have you noticed how those who make the pursuit of happiness their supreme goal become the most miserable people? Nothing can compare with the happiness that God gives to those who, like Paul, 'make it our goal to please him' (2 Corinthians 5:9).

I can still hear the passionate voice of a senior missionary as he addressed a leaders' conference. He was speaking on Jesus' parable of the tenants in Mark 12:1–12. Do you recall how the owner of the vineyard finally sent his son to collect his payment? The tenants then said to one another, 'This is the heir. Come, let's kill him, and the inheritance will be ours.' The speaker pressed home this question: 'Who owns the vineyard?' We all know the answer. The question is, do we act as if we do? Do we acknowledge his rights? Or do we think of our gifts and ministry as if we were the owners rather than the trustees? This is not a lesson we learn once and for all in Bible college, or in our first term of service. It is something we need to come to terms with over and over again, as servants of Christ; something we need to take ourselves in hand about; something we need to ask others to pray for, for us. Our commitment is to Christ, and not to our own fulfilment. This commitment will be tested time and again.

> **This commitment will be tested time and again.**

Learning a different drumbeat

Some cultures are as pressured and as 'driven' as our own. Others have lifestyles which travel at a very different pace. We may think them inefficient, and in many ways they are. But let us not be quite so quick to judge. We should not overlook the weaknesses of our own backgrounds. Those from slower cultures will perceive things we miss. They may think us deficient, unable to measure our pace and get more out of life's various experiences.

To the Westerner, time can be all-important. It is measurable – in hours, minutes, seconds. It can be saved or wasted. Perhaps those in our host country think more about its value than its length: what you do with it is what matters. They may rate occasion and relationships more highly, and may be the better for that. We will find ourselves being enriched, and gaining fresh insights, if we adapt our pace a little to their drumbeat. There are things we can learn here.

I recall some shrewd observations from three women missionaries who crossed the Gobi Desert five times by horse and cart. They were a remarkable trio, by any standards. Addressing a crowd in London just before returning to the nomads and traders of the Silk Road for their final term of service, one of them said this:

> At home, all is for speed, but the ancient roads, with their three miles per hour, are better suited for the great business of preaching the gospel. Christ joined himself to two discouraged disciples on the road, and the talk was about great things. The great question of the road is 'Where have you come from and where are you going?' Think what you lose by speed. You can't talk of these great and everlasting subjects when speed is the passion.[2]

---

2. Mildred Cable, and Francesca and Eva French, known simply as 'The Trio' were missionaries with the China Inland Mission. Mildred Cable was speaking here. Anything written by them or about them is worth reading. Search them out in secondhand bookshops or on Amazon.

All this can mean that the process of gaining acceptance in another culture is slower too. One frustration can be the delay in finding opportunities for ministry. We set off to our new sphere filled with energy and zeal, eager to get stuck in. But instead of doors opening, they remain stubbornly closed. Instead of our gifts and experience being recognised, we are left on the sidelines.

> **The great question of the road is 'Where have you come from and where are you going?'**

We are tempted to think we would have been more useful if we had stayed at home. We might have had a fulfilling role pastoring a church or leading a youth ministry, working among people we knew and understood. We may find ourselves resentful, feeling that the church leaders in our host country must lack discernment, or they would recognise straight away what we can do for them. We can even find ourselves despising them. Our emotions can run high. Is this the price we have to pay? Is that reasonable? Did we come to this country just to vegetate? What's going on?

> **Did we come to this country just to vegetate?**

Even at home it takes time to become accepted and recognised in a new situation. Perhaps we are experiencing nothing more than that. This feature of change of role is common to every move in life. But if we haven't experienced it before, it can come as a shock, and if we are struggling with a new language at the same time, it can be extremely difficult to handle. It can take us by surprise and be very frustrating. It is one of the real tests of our willingness to let God be God in our lives, and let him control the way he uses our gifts.

Added to this, the cultures we find in many developing countries have very different attitudes to youth and age from those in our home countries. Many nations have a greater respect for age and experience, and may be less inclined to make way for younger people. We need to respect their cultural distinctives and be patient with the process. In the process, we will come to appreciate our host culture more and learn valuable lessons.

> **Many nations may be less inclined to make way for younger people.**

We need to be aware of how we come across. Perhaps without realising it, we may seem patronising. We may even be perceived as showing national pride. It is much harder for us to avoid this than we sometimes realise. National pride is a subtle and insidious thing. It is so easy for us to behave in ways that convey a message of superiority without meaning to. No surprise, then, if people don't rush to make much of us, or to give us positions of prominence!

Whatever the factors at play, if we are to be truly useful to those we serve, we need to learn lessons of patience and humility. Is it our 'right' to have our gifts and ministry recognised? Well, no, it isn't. And in the end, God's pace in this process is best and will lead to greater effectiveness.

George Whitefield, one of the great preachers in the 18th-century spiritual awakening in the UK and the USA, was an unwearying activist. Often, when he had preached himself into the ground and was on the point of collapse, he would find himself fired up by a fresh opportunity, with all his energies restored! In his ministry he crossed the Atlantic thirteen times, but not in a jumbo jet cruising at 570 mph, of course. His travel was in a sailing ship, on a journey that took weeks, not hours.

The activist in him seized the opportunity of preaching to everyone on board! But when he had done all that he could of that, he had only reading and writing left to spend the days on. Initially, he chafed at this 'loss' of time. But at one point he records in his journal, 'I have learned that the reaper is not wasting his time when he is whetting his scythe.' He learned to see the benefit of God's 'sharpening' and to submit to it with a more patient spirit.

We could do worse than learn from George Whitefield, when our 'journey' to ministry opportunities seems slow. Sharpen the scythe!

Why don't they do things my way?

We all start off thinking that the way we handle things is better than the way other cultures do. Perhaps we even believe there is no other way of doing things! We soon realise otherwise. Experience brings home to us that other cultures solve some common human problems very differently. Wisdom may teach us that in some cases their answers are better than ours. And sometimes, of course, they simply get it wrong – just as we all do.

> **We all think that the way we handle things is better.**

These differences can be instructive; they can also be frustrating. We can find frustration in watching the way they make decisions or resolve conflict (including the way

> **People in many two-thirds-world cultures are less confrontational than Westerners.**

they handle church discipline). Typically, people in many two-thirds-world cultures are less confrontational than Westerners, and this comes out clearly in areas of conflict. Sometimes it will seem to a Western observer that the issue is simply being avoided. When a matter is taken forward, progress can seem intolerably slow. Our customs in these areas are sometimes better, sometimes worse – or sometimes just different! When we first encounter these differences we would be wise to suspend our judgment at first, and watch and listen. Stephen and Jill's story may be an example.[3]

Stephen and Jill's story

Stephen and Jill met at Bible College, where both were preparing for long-term cross-cultural service. Their first year abroad was marked by good progress with language and culture acquisition, and promising ministry in the urban environment. People remarked on Stephen's excellent relationships with the nationals. At the end of that year they were allocated to a rural Bible College teaching post. Some doubted the wisdom of this allocation, as there had been a history of misunderstandings between the mission and church leaders in that community. But they threw themselves into the work with great zeal and early days were trouble-free.

Very soon, Stephen was asked to take on a

---

3. Stephen and Jill are fictitious, but the story, while not an exact record of any situation, is a true reflection of many.

more senior role in the college, which he did. This was not without its strains, however, and it soon put him under pressure. Then the difficulties began.

Embarking on this ministry brought him face to face with local realities. Stephen is a gifted and able man, and like many such people, he sets high standards for himself – and for others! Some students couldn't match them, and they resented his position. Some decisions had been taken by national administrative staff, which he felt further undermined the drive for good academic standards, and he was not happy about this. He felt that problems needed to be addressed, and he set about doing so. The tensions increased, and included student protests.

Missionary colleagues were divided, some supporting him in his position, others feeling he was impatient and not sufficiently respecting of the church leadership. This probably reflected the range of personalities and cultures within the mission team as much as it did the issues! National leaders, too, were divided, some opposing him while others continued to respect and value him.

The situation reached stalemate, and attempts at reconciliation proved fruitless. As in many such situations, there were probably rights and wrongs on both sides, and the conflict might well have

> **There were probably rights and wrongs on both sides.**

been as much due to 'style' as to 'substance'. In the end, Stephen and Jill, hurt and confused, were designated to a different situation. Time will tell what lessons can be learned from the whole painful episode.

Perhaps Stephen should have been slower to evaluate how his host culture was functioning. Our first mistake is often not one of judgment, but of understanding wrongly. We jump to make value judgments on how an unfamiliar culture 'works' before we've truly understood what's going on. Let's work hard at being slow to come to conclusions.

Stephen's experience probably also illustrates another truth. People from different Western cultures differ from each other! So life can be further complicated by working in a multinational team of missionaries. New missionaries are very aware of the obviously unfamiliar features of their host culture, and are not surprised by them. What they are less prepared for are the differences between Canadian and Australian, British and American and so on.

The struggle comes when we think we know what should be done but can do nothing about it. It may be inappropriate for us, as guests, to appear to criticise our hosts. If we do offer suggestions, they may be ignored or resented. It can be even more difficult when we find that we have to follow lines we disagree with. If the issue is one of principle, then the right course of action for us may be straightforward, if costly. More often, however, the issue is not as clear cut.

A common example is the area of legalism. We may be astonished to find that a style of dress which is completely acceptable in our home country is frowned on in the national churches. It may be as basic as wearing sandals instead of shoes, or an open-necked shirt instead of a collar and tie. In these circumstances, do you have the freedom to follow your own preferences, or do you conform?

Do you have the freedom to follow your own preferences, or do you conform?

If the other person's position is just mildly 'narrow' (like style of dress), we may decide the wiser course is simply to accept it. Paul's encouragement to us to submit to one another would apply (Ephesians 5:21). But the decision becomes more difficult if we feel it undermines the gospel (as Paul concluded Peter's behaviour in Antioch did: see Galatians 2). Toeing the line can be the right and gracious way forward, but compromising the gospel would not be. What do we do when one person sees something as an issue of conscience while the other thinks it is comparatively unimportant? Paul's principle of 'the weaker brother' then applies (see 1 Corinthians 8:1–13; 10:23–33). Let each hold to his own view, Paul would teach us, but the one who is 'free' needs to be careful not in any way to put pressure on the other person to do something he regards as wrong. In all of this, the principle seems to be love, and concern for another, without becoming tyrannised by anyone's opinions. Great principles, but not easy to put into practice!

Matters can also be aggravated by differing attitudes to authority. Expressing a different opinion may be quite acceptable at home. Christians in our host country, however, might see it as disloyal or insubordinate. This same issue of authority can arise in relationships with senior missionary colleagues, especially those in authority over you. You may think they have attitudes to authority that disappeared ten or twenty years ago in your home country. You may feel they have conformed too much to the national churches' views, and have failed to promote biblical teaching on freedom. But we would probably be wise to recognise that our own cultures have moved very far from the biblical standards for accepting authority, and are not necessarily a good guide.

How do we react in these situations? What 'rights' can we exercise? Be sure of this: we will meet situations where we find ourselves perplexed. In fact situations like these may be among the most baffling we will ever encounter. Whatever the issue, in most cases the right course will be to say less than we think, and to accept authority more readily than we would like to, or are used to. Can we do that, for the sake of Christ?

> **We will meet situations where we find ourselves perplexed.**

Has God changed his mind?

We have thought about opportunities that are slow in coming, and the cost of waiting for them. We have looked at unwelcome constraints on our ministry, and the cost of submission. Perhaps there's another even more demanding scenario.

I recall a missionary couple sitting in my office. Through traumatic circumstances, and through no fault of their own, they had had to leave their work in Africa and return home. In anguish the man cried out, 'Why, Lord, did you give us the vision and not allow us to fulfil it?' It seemed so pointless, all the years of preparation, the years of acquiring the language and culture – for nothing. I felt with them, and

> **It seemed so pointless, all the years of preparation.**

I could hear the question going round and round in their heads. 'If we have made sacrifices and faced costs for this, should we not be allowed to have a decent stab at it?'

Fortunately, as elsewhere in this book, we might here be looking at something that is not common. But it does happen to some, and we can prepare ourselves for it. We need to lay down in our hearts and minds a foundation of trust in a God who does all things well; a God who is our heavenly Father; a God whose every action in the lives of his children is marked by his wisdom and love; a God whose wise and loving treatment of his children can be very mystifying at the time, but – as history shows – is vindicated by events. (See for example the 'Lessons from China' opposite.)

In England in the 18th century, the great preacher John Wesley, the founder of Methodism, came across some words written a hundred years earlier to focus people's thoughts on 'making a covenant with God'. Wesley took up the words and instituted in the Methodist churches an annual 'Covenant service' at the start of each year. Many Methodist churches around the world still use this. Perhaps its words will help us lay that foundation in our own thoughts. I leave them in their slightly older language; the first paragraph is instruction, the second a response in prayer, and the third a declaration of contentment that God be God.

> **Christ has many services to be done; some are easy, others are difficult; some bring honour, others bring reproach; some are suitable to our natural inclinations and temporal interests, others are contrary to both. In some we may please Christ and please ourselves, in others we cannot please Christ except by denying**

Lessons from China

In 1949 the Communists came to power in China, and over a fifth of the world's population suddenly came under Communist rule. In the hundred years up to then, it had been possible, though often dangerous, to travel in the country, and to preach Christ. Now that freedom had disappeared.

Over the next two years all missionaries were withdrawn. What a painful departure it was, but there was no alternative, as Chinese Christians associating with foreigners soon came under particular scrutiny from the government. Missionaries sensed that their Christian friends, whom they had nurtured and mentored, would suffer greatly. As they sailed home to Europe, North America, Australia, they could hardly believe what God had allowed to happen. How would the Church survive?

Chairman Mao would have loved to stamp the Church out, but he did not have that power. Through the years that followed it was sometimes hard to find out what was happening, not least during the dark days of the Cultural Revolution. But Christians round the world prayed, and God heard their prayers. Through all its suffering, the Chinese Church not only survived, but it grew.

Throughout the 1930s and 1940s the Holy Spirit had been working in unusual ways among university students. The China Inter-Varsity Fellowship was soon the largest evangelical student movement in the world, and in 1947 it became a founding member of the fledgling IFES. In universities right across the land, leaders were being trained for the Church which would soon have to meet secretly. Today that Church is the largest evangelical community in the world, and the Holy Spirit continues to work in remarkable ways among students.

One of the missions serving in China was the China Inland Mission. In 1952 its Council met to decide what to do. Was the work founded by Hudson Taylor now complete in God's eyes? No, they sensed, it wasn't. This was when the mission reformed, becoming what is now OMF International; those missionaries who had left China now sailed for Japan, Thailand, the Philippines and other East Asian countries. They worked first among the Chinese communities, and then more widely with the Japanese, the Thai, the Filipinos... The Church in most of these places is now established under national leadership; in others it is still small and struggling.

Who owns the vineyard? God owns the vineyard. The remarkable account of the suffering and glory of the Chinese Church is rich in lessons on this. God is sovereign, and in his providence he places his workers where he chooses.

ourselves. Yet the power to do all these things is assuredly given us in Christ, who strengthens us.

I am no longer my own but yours. Put me to what you will, rank me with whom you will; put me to doing, put me to suffering; let me be employed for you or laid aside for you, exalted for you or brought low for you; let me be full, let me be empty, let me have all things, let me have nothing; I freely and wholeheartedly yield all things to your pleasure and disposal.

And now, glorious and blessed God, Father, Son and Holy Spirit, you are mine and I am yours. So be it. And the covenant now made on earth, let it be ratified in heaven. Amen.

Don't rush on. Take some time to reflect on these words. The prayer is a very searching one. If this is to be our covenant with God, let us make it that. And perhaps look over the prayer as Wesley urged the Methodists to do, regularly.

Do we believe God owns the vineyard?

In the next chapter you will meet Lloyd Porter, who serves with Operation Mobilisation in Russia. When Lloyd first thought about joining OM, his friends protested. They said he was already far too useful in Christian work in Australia. It would be a waste of his gifts to pass by the opportunities (summer camps, for example) in which God was already using him.

Lloyd is not alone in that experience. The people God calls abroad are certain to be active in his service wherever they are. They are the people who will be missed! Yes, there are disadvantages in moving into another culture:

the loss of time while we learn another language, the painful process of adapting, the years spent in learning lessons and making mistakes. We keep finding ourselves drawn back to that critical question: who owns the vineyard?

And let us always have in our thinking that gospel plea of Paul in Romans 10:14,15: 'How, then, can they call on the one they have not believed in? And how can they believe in the one of whom they have not heard? And how can they hear without someone preaching to them? And how can they preach unless they are sent?' Someone must go. If everyone through the centuries had listened to reasons for not going, the Church would still be confined to the Middle East!

> **If everyone through the centuries had listened to reasons for not going, the church would still be confined to the Middle East!**

God has done many wonderful things through the lives of dedicated men and women whom he buried in what seem to us to be unpromising situations. These people took seriously Jesus' teaching that when a grain of wheat 'dies' it bears fruit (John 12:24). Jesus goes on to say, 'The man who loves his life will lose it, while the man who hates his life in this world will keep it for eternal life.' There are men and women who have believed that divine paradox, and their lives have proved it true.

I was moved recently by a searching little booklet written by Ajith Fernando, Director of Sri Lanka Youth for Christ.[4] He recounts the training he gives to his staff:

---

4. *An Authentic Servant: The Marks of a Spiritual Leader* by Ajith Fernando (IFES/OMF)

Christian ministers are those who first get their
strength from God, and then go into the world
to get bashed around. Then they come back,
get their strength from God, and go back into
the world to get bashed again. That is our life.
We get strength, then we go and get bashed,
get strength, go get bashed, get strength...

Christian ministry is a demanding and costly calling, but
the 'well done' will be worth hearing.

CHAPTER 4

Money and standards of living

L ife in Oz can be great for a young man with a good education and a good job. That was Lloyd's experience before God called him to move into another culture. His story touches on one of the obvious costs of serving abroad – money! Moving to live in another culture often brings with it a lowered standard of living, especially if we're going to be working with a Christian agency such as a missionary society. Taking the plunge and accepting a drop in living standards is one thing. Working through the issues when we face them in the first months abroad is another. Seeing our contemporaries enjoying increasing prosperity is yet another!

Lloyd's story

Lloyd was an MK ('missionary kid'), or what is known now as a 'third-culture' child. He grew up in Kashmir in India and his family moved back to Australia when he was eleven. He qualified as a Quantity Surveyor and landed a great job. He loved his work. But it was only a few months after his final exams that he felt the Lord was leading him to Eastern Europe to serve short-term with Operation Mobilisation.

Lloyd remembers opening his Bible at Hebrews 11. 'I was challenged by Abraham's story. He was called and obeyed, not knowing where he was going. (Hebrews 11:8). It was as if I had a choice to stay back – or step out. And I stepped out, not knowing then what it would mean. I have never regretted it.' Obedience had a cost, however: he'd just bought his own apartment in Perth, he had a secure job, and he loved his surfy car!

> **He'd just bought his own apartment in Perth, had a secure job, and loved his surfy car!**

As the months in Eastern Europe passed, Lloyd knew he had to think about the future. 'The time in Siberia was exciting – people were being saved, a church was planted. The whole week was a round of Russian Bible studies and prayer meetings, and street evangelism! But through all this I still didn't know if God wanted me to stay there. Part of me was drawn by the thought of going back to Perth and pursuing a lucrative career. But I kept thinking of Hebrews 11, and wondered what I was aiming for. What was God's best?'

One hard question had been the issue of church support. Although his church had supported him in prayer, they hadn't stood behind him financially. How would he survive more years in mission without that support?

'During this amazing time in Siberia, the economy in Australia went through a shaky patch.

How would he survive in mission without support?

Interest rates went up and rents fell. Back home my parents were watching my bank balance dwindle with not enough rent coming in to cover the outgoings. The flat was finally sold at a greatly reduced price and instead of an asset and a bank balance, I suddenly had a debt of $8,000. It was hard to lose that security and what I had worked for over several years.'

Still reeling from the news, Lloyd was wondering, 'What on earth do I do now, Lord?' Then God spoke to him again through Hebrews 11, and Moses' choice to follow the Lord. So Lloyd decided that he would go home, work to pay off the debt – and then come back to his beloved Russia. Soon after he decided this, his church wrote to say they'd like to start supporting him financially!

In some ways that period looked like a costly two years. Lloyd lost his own home and 'secure' future, gaining instead a debt, and longer term, a call to a deeply unstable country. But he also saw how the Lord walked through this time with him. And he has now been able to pay off his debts and return to Russia.

That was in the early 1990s. Lloyd is still in Russia, now married to Katherine, and they have two daughters. Katherine's launching pad for ministry in Eastern Europe was a degree in

English from Cambridge. I could go on to tell of her call to mission as she watched the Berlin Wall come down; of the way she then stayed back in the UK to nurse her dying grandmother; and of her joy in being part of the first evangelistic outreach in Albania for nearly half a century when people clamoured to hear the gospel.

Lloyd and Katherine moved to St Petersburg when Lloyd became the Field Leader for OM in Russia. They are now seeing Russians go overseas to serve in places such as Zimbabwe, Nepal and on the OM ships. There remain plenty of challenges still each day for both of them – but God remains faithful to those he has called.

The wealthy West

Until we've been in contact with two-thirds-world poverty, we easily fail to grasp the gulf between the world's 'haves' and 'have-nots'. We may know in theory that a lot of the world is less affluent than we are, but often it doesn't sink in until we see it for ourselves.

Let us at least note the facts in passing. The World Bank[5] issues a comprehensive Annual World Development Report. It shows, for example, the Gross National Product (GNP) per capita of countries, both western and 'two-thirds-world'. Now of course these are just the bare figures. To make valid comparisons you need to take all sorts of factors into account. But the

> **The extremes we see there must mean something!**

5. www.worldbank.com

extremes we see there must mean something! There is obviously the most enormous difference between what we take for granted in Europe and North America, on the one hand, and how men and women live in much of the rest of the world. We enjoy an affluence way beyond the imagining of millions of our fellow human beings.

> **Millions live full and rewarding lives on a fraction of the incomes we expect.**

It's worth putting any puny sacrifices we might make against that backdrop. It's also useful to remember that, while many live in the most appalling and tragic poverty in the world, there are also millions who live full and rewarding lives on a fraction of the incomes we expect in the West. 'Needs' can be relative, and what we regard as needs may well be unimaginable luxury to others.

How far will my living standards drop?

These world realities mean that some adjustment of lifestyle shouldn't surprise us. If we are going abroad to take up a normal professional job, it may be possible to live about as comfortably as we do at home, depending on the country. But in many places the conditions simply will not allow for the same comforts and conveniences. There won't be a Next or a Macy's down the road. You won't have a choice of TV channels. People may never have heard of your favourite food. And in less trivial ways you will be aware that you're not at home. Some places are primitive, and some are tough. There's no escaping that. Life won't be the same. That can be exciting too, of course.

You may be weighing up the possibility of going

Your expected income is unlikely to place you in the annual lists of the top 200 earners!

overseas with a mission or some other Christian agency. If so, it won't have escaped your attention that your expected income is unlikely to place you in the annual lists of the top 200 earners! You'll be facing the reality of a reduced income, lower – sometimes much lower – than you might take for granted in your home country. If it is paid in sterling or dollars, it may translate quite well into the soft currencies of a two-thirds-world country. But you will not have an employer paying a percentage of your salary into a pension fund, as most graduates in secular employment now expect. (Most mission agencies do make pension provision, but it will not compare with the pension some of your contemporaries will eventually be drawing.)

There is something else to take into account. The standard of living that we can maintain on our missionary allowance may still leave a great gap between us and those around us in our host country. Even missionaries may appear wealthy to most nationals! This raises some tough questions for us, if we want to have genuine friendships with Christians around us and want our

Our missionary allowance may still leave a great gap between us and those around us.

ministry to be effective. If we are working alongside Christian nationals, how do we express our fellowship? As a rule, they will not expect us to live completely at their level. That is usually unwise and often impossible. But how great a discrepancy can our ministry tolerate?

68

Do we need to deny ourselves things to go some way towards bridging the gulf between what we can afford and how the people we work amongst live? These are agonising questions, and questions that may not have one absolutely right answer. But we should note the concern, and the fact that some of the most sensitive missionaries believe these are questions that we will need to answer. Once again we find ourselves battling with the issue of 'rights'. Is it not my right to live comfortably, enjoying the rewards my gifts, training and experience can receive?

Four ways money works

Let's look at some of the ways in which money 'works' in our culture. These may help identify the questions we will need to work through.

1. An indicator of how we are valued

In our Western cultures money is widely seen as an indicator of how we are valued in our jobs. This is not necessarily wrong, and in fact it has been a feature of all cash economies, reaching back into biblical times. So increased output, greater responsibilities or greater risk-taking are rewarded with more money. While some people dislike this pattern, alternatives don't seem to work very well. Generally speaking, this is the way things function in our secular working environments.

It takes a mental shift of gear to get out of this mindset, and working for most donation-supported organisations will call for such a shift in thinking. We soon come to understand that in such organisations we do not get what we or others think we might deserve. Seniority may or may not be recognised with an increased salary or allowance, but in cases where it is, it is unlikely to be a significant 'jump', and will not equate with similar levels of responsibility in the business world or in the public sector. Merit and 'rights' don't come into it! Money is given to the mission for its ministry, and there is usually not enough to make the most of the opportunities. Accepting this way of thinking about money is one of the costs to be faced.

2. A measure of success

For some people it is making money that is the challenge. For them, it is not money itself that is the lure, or what money can buy, but simply the drive to succeed. So money-making becomes the measure of their success in running their business. It's like winning a game. These people usually play Monopoly with the same vigour, and often win! Money, for them, is more a matter of fascination than of covetousness.

Here again, we aren't looking at something that is evil in itself. There are many legitimate fascinations in life. But there are dangers. These things can become obsessive, and any obsession has its dangers. In advising the Corinthian church about the uncertainties of their times, Paul uses an interesting word. He writes:

> *What I mean, brothers, is that the time is short. From now on those who have wives should live as if they had none; those who mourn,*

*as if they did not; those who
are happy, as if they were
not; those who buy
something, as if it were not
theirs to keep; those who use
the things of the world, as if
not engrossed in them.*
(1 Corinthians 7:29–31)

The word translated 'engrossed' means something like 'overusing'. Paul is saying that there is a legitimate involvement with 'the things of this world', but that we can become preoccupied with them. They can loom too large in our thinking and compete with our commitment to other values and other loyalties.

3. A route to status symbols

Money is a key to all sorts of status symbols, pleasures and recreations. It's what money can buy that is the lure. Some of these can be legitimate; for the Christian, some are a snare. Jesus warns against the dangerous distraction that we can find in 'worries, riches and pleasures' (Luke 8:14). They can stifle the work of God's Word in our lives. And we find that, when our mind is so filled with these things, we never have enough. However wealthy we are, and however easily we can buy what we want, we want more.

The Christian life is not a call to asceticism. God gives most of us more than we need, and to some of us he entrusts a great deal. Money can be put to good uses, and God calls some to earn big salaries and give to mission – George Verwer refers to such people as the 'unsung heroes'!

> **God calls some to earn big salaries and give to mission.**

How else would God's work be supported? Paul – like his master – never condemns wealth as such, nor does he teach us that all Christians should dispose of all their possessions. But he does warn of the dangers of wealth.

Paul writes to Timothy: 'People who want to get rich fall into temptation and a trap and into many foolish and harmful desires that plunge men into ruin and destruction. For the love of money is a root of all kinds of evil. Some people, eager for money, have wandered from the faith and pierced themselves with many griefs' (1 Timothy 6:9,10). A staggering statement! But note his choice of words: '... want to get rich ... love of money ... eager for money'. He is warning against the desire for money, not its possession. A poor man who dreams of wealth may be more in view here than a rich man who is not a prisoner to his wealth.

Later in the same letter, Paul has a word for those who are wealthy. Timothy is to 'Command those who are rich in this present world not to be arrogant nor to put their hope in wealth, which is so uncertain, but to put their hope in God, who richly provides us with everything for our enjoyment. Command them to do good, to be rich in good deeds, and to be generous and willing to share' (1 Timothy 6:17,18). Here again it is the wrong attitude to wealth that he warns against, and its selfish use.

4. A key to security

The fourth way in which money functions in our cultures is for security. We earn money to provide food, shelter, clothing, holidays, children's education. We look ahead to retirement and make provision for a time when we will no longer be able to earn. Unemployment creates anxiety because we fear we may not be able to meet our needs and those of our family.

72

For some people thinking of going overseas, this is one of the big battles. Will they have enough? Will their family and children be adequately provided for? Our parents can go through the same struggles, whether they are Christians or not. Grandparents can be very anxious about their grandchildren! And that is understandable. It is natural – and good – to feel a sense of responsibility for the wellbeing of our families.

Perhaps security is the most sensitive of the roles that money plays, and one we need to explore further.

Money and security

What is the Bible's perspective on security? Note the words of Paul quoted above: 'wealth is uncertain'. Look at Lloyd's story again, at the start of this chapter. He made what he thought was careful and adequate provision, but unforeseen changes in the economy landed him in debt. The financial future was not as sure and predictable as he had thought. And life is full of stories like that. This isn't to say that we shouldn't be prudent in planning our finances. I believe we should.

> **The financial future was not as sure and predictable as he had thought.**

But our ultimate security isn't to be found in our bank balance or our pension plans.

The other side of the equation is that, while wealth may be uncertain, God's care is certain. Jesus leaves us in no doubt about that in this striking passage from the Sermon on the Mount:

> *Do not store up for
> yourselves treasures on earth,*

*where moth and rust destroy,
and where thieves break in
and steal. But store up for
yourselves treasures in
heaven, where moth and rust
do not destroy, and where
thieves do not break in and
steal. For where your
treasure is, there your heart
will be also.*

*Therefore I tell you, do
not worry about your life,
what you will eat or drink; or
about your body, what you
will wear. Is not life more
important than food, and the
body more important than
clothes? Look at the birds of
the air; they do not sow or
reap or store away in barns,
and yet your heavenly Father
feeds them. Are you not
much more valuable than
they? Who of you by
worrying can add a single
hour to his life?*

*And why do you worry
about clothes? See how the
lilies of the field grow. They
do not labour or spin. Yet I
tell you that not even
Solomon in all his splendour
was dressed like one of
these. If that is how God*

clothes the grass of the field,
which is here today and
tomorrow is thrown into the
fire, will he not much more
clothe you, O you of little
faith? So do not worry,
saying, 'What shall we eat?'
or 'What shall we drink?' or
'What shall we wear?' For
the pagans run after all these
things, and your heavenly
Father knows that you need
them. But seek first his
kingdom and his
righteousness, and all these
things will be given to you as
well. Therefore do not worry
about tomorrow, for
tomorrow will worry about
itself. Each day has enough
trouble of its own.
(Matthew 6:19–21, 25–34)

Jesus tells his disciples not to be anxious but to trust in a Father's care. He illustrates God's care from nature, and teaches the futility of worry. But to receive a command not to be anxious isn't very easy to handle. It's not easy just to 'switch off' fear or anxiety. So he first gives them the focus to their thinking that will make it possible. He talks of 'storing up treasures in heaven'. He calls us to have a focus on heaven, not this world, in our ambitions and aspirations. Here, 'heaven' speaks to us of God's realm, of his rule. It is the place where God's will is perfectly done. It speaks to us of the invisible things which are in fact more substantial and enduring than the visible things that seem so real and lasting to us.

The invisible things are in fact more substantial and enduring than the visible things.

In effect, it's almost as if Jesus is teaching that if we get heaven and earth in perspective, his commands to us to be trusting and fearless are really quite easy! Certainly, if we are wrestling with God's call to serve him overseas and make financial sacrifices, this is a good place for us to spend time, in our thinking and praying.

God's plans for us are that some – not many! – are entrusted with wealth. Whether we are wealthy or not, we can never lay claim to wealth. We have no rights to it. But as his child you do have a right to trust in the Father's care. He has promised us that. And that gives more security than all the gold in Fort Knox.

Do you fear that God may be calling you to something too hard for you? Let's bring the curtain down on this chapter with the words of Jim Elliot, the martyr missionary to the Auca Indians:

He is no fool who gives what he cannot keep to gain what he cannot lose.

CHAPTER 5

Career prospects

Tim and Emily Hay have recently moved to Belgium from the UK. Here's their story:

Tim grew up in Brussels, Emily in the UK. Tim qualified as a lawyer and worked in the area of criminal defence; Emily as a speech and language therapist. Both were doing well and enjoying their careers. Tim speaks three languages, with a working knowledge of a fourth. His legal background, together with language skills, could have opened up interesting career moves. But Tim and Emily both sensed the Lord calling them into a very different future.

Both had grown spiritually during their own student days in UK Christian Unions, and both had a deep desire to see Christ's name honoured in the university world. As they talked with older friends and with their pastor, they began to see how their gifts could be pressed into service in Belgium. Based in Brussels, they now work alongside the French-speaking Groupes Bibliques Universitaires (IFES), leading a small international team. Their team is pioneering an evangelistic ministry to international students, many of whom come from countries which are hostile to the gospel.

Tim and Emily are not far from home. The culture is still Western, and they have good language skills. Their two boys, Luke and Daniel, will become increasingly bilingual as they enter local schools.

Most Belgian students live at home or travel home at weekends. The GBU groups are small, often with only six or seven members. Universities are either Catholic or secular; neither is keen on evangelical student groups, and the secular universities prohibit any advertising or use of facilities. It is sometimes hard for Tim and Emily not to share the discouragement of the handful of Christian students.

> **Secular universities prohibit any advertising or use of facilities.**

Tim had completed a year at the Cornhill Training Course, with its emphasis on developing preaching skills. Could they not just have continued in their careers with Tim using these skills from time to time at weekends?

Some people might think Tim and Emily have wasted their training and abilities. They might argue that the skills they have gained should be ploughed back into the country which paid for their education. The plain sense of that argument seems to hold water, but only in a simple arithmetical kind of framework.

Others will say that as God has given them these gifts, they have the right to use them to best advantage, however they press them into service.

This is God's world

How do we respond in either case? Let's start by sketching out some of the biblical framework for how we ought to think of our work in this world. We should note first that there is something of an ambiguity in how the Bible views the world.

On the one hand, we are taught that it is God's world. He made it, he owns it and he rules it. Our sinfulness doesn't change that. It is now a world under judgment, yet still he loves it and cares for it. 'He has compassion on all he has made,' says the Psalmist (Psalm 145:9). He sets in place – and deposes – the rulers of the nations (Romans 13:1). As the Dutch theologian Abraham Kuyper once said: 'In the total expanse of human life, there is no square inch of which Jesus Christ may not say, "That is mine!" ' And Christians have generally agreed that the commission to develop and care for the world which God gave in the opening chapters of Genesis is still in force. We have made a mess of that task, and still do, but the job remains ours.

Education, industry, medicine, politics, law, environmental protection, whatever – all these play a part in God's ordering of the world. And we can pursue all these as service to God, as outworkings of his 'common grace' to the world. So, if that is where God calls us, there is value and dignity before him in a career in the world. Having this

> **There is value and dignity in a career.**

grasp of its being God's world means we can see the whole of our lives as part of that high aspiration to please him in all we do (see 2 Corinthians 5:9).

Of course, because we are a fallen race, we make a mess of things. By our nature as sinful human beings, we spoil the work we do, and we also corrupt our motives in what we do. So what is intended to be the service of God our Creator becomes a means of self-promotion at the expense of others and of God's world. Our godly service soon becomes nothing more worthy than selfish ambition stamped with the logo of the company or the emblem of the college. Careerism rules OK. Instead of being in the service of God, our career and our gifts become our gods. But we are told to keep ourselves from idols (1 John 5:21).

And that brings us to the other side of the ambiguity.

This is a fallen world

The other way in which the Bible sees 'the world' is not as the wonderful creation of God, but as the sphere in which rebellion continues to be played out by creatures against their Creator. This is the 'world' that we are told will hate us because it hated Jesus (John 15:18). This is the 'world' that we are encouraged to see as transient. This is the 'world' we are warned to avoid, not to love (1 John 2:15). This 'world' is the spirit that can seduce us into total absorption in our careers, and make us more concerned to be admired by others than approved by God.

It is not for nothing that John Stott's exposition of the Sermon on the Mount is entitled 'Christian Counter-culture'. Those who are Christ's and have God's Spirit in them belong to a different sphere. We have a different 'citizenship' (Philippians 3:20). While we accept the call to serve in this world, we are not of this world. And no matter how much we might earn the appreciation and admiration of 'the world', sooner or later – if we live consistently with our faith – people will find something unusual about us. No matter how fully we play a role in this world, they will see that we march to a different drum. These two aspects of

the world put us in some sort of tension. Christians haven't always managed to keep the balance between affirming the world and denying it. Both find their place in the Bible, but through the years the Church has often gone to one extreme or the other.

Yet to grasp this 'in-between' or 'both-and' position is wonderfully liberating. It is part of the freedom we find in Christ. Those around us, often claiming to be free, are imprisoned in the world's rat race. Christ enables us to be involved in this world while not being 'engrossed' in it. (See the comment on 1 Corinthians 7 in the last chapter.) This gives us a framework for seeing how both going abroad and serving at home can equally find a place in how God uses us.

The potter and the clay

Of course, when we see our work as part of our service to God, certain things follow. He is Lord! The biblical picture that sets this out clearly is that of the potter and the clay. The potter chooses what kind of pot to make with each piece of clay, and the pot isn't entitled to object! We are his clay. He then has the authority to redirect our service into whichever channels he chooses. He knows what is the best use of the gifts he has given us. It is not 'interference' on his part if he re-allocates us to service overseas.

Sometimes that call is to use the same gifts and training that we have been exercising in our home country. For example, he calls some to be 'tent-makers', to take up secular positions in other countries. This may be the best route for reaching places closed to more explicit forms of Christian service. As 'Christian professionals', we might find ourselves playing a role very similar to the one we were doing in our home countries. And alongside the opportunities we have of bringing the message of Christ to our host country, we are able to use our skills to make a contribution to its development, and its people's wellbeing.

> **As 'Christian professionals' we might play a role very similar to the one in our home countries.**

On the other hand, God has the prerogative to change our direction more radically, and bring out other gifts in us. He might steer us into spheres where our past training seems quite irrelevant. Sometimes our friends, family or church leaders can find that hard to accept. It can seem a waste, a misuse of resources, a squandering of opportunities. But God is in charge, and his use of his resources is governed by his wisdom and power. Wonderfully, we usually find that more of the lessons learned in our previous occupation carry over into our new sphere than we would ever have imagined.

Do you know how to fail?

As I have talked with missionaries from the West and the new West, who have been willing to serve in hard situations, I have heard stories of stark contrasts between their present roles and the stimulation and fulfilment they found back in their home countries. There was no sense of success any more; no coming home at the end of the day feeling they had achieved something.

I remember talking with a missionary doctor in an outpatients' clinic in a developing country in Africa. He drew my attention to one of the patients and explained her condition. What could be done for her? With the facilities available in his home country – a great deal. With their current facilities – nothing! She would soon be dead. For a professional who is used to being able to save lives by drawing on high-tech up-to-date drugs and equipment, that's hard to accept. It's a blow to one's professionalism.

This sense of failure is not uncommon amongst those who move from high professional standards at home to the conditions of deprivation that are all too common. That can be true of any form of Christian service, of course. We need God to make us less sure of our own resources and more reliant on his. One 'tent-maker' in a tough situation tells how, when talking to potential fellow-workers, he asks them, 'Do you know how to fail?'

> **We need God to make us less sure of our own resources.**

It's a Lordship issue

Another potential loss arises for those who come to re-enter their profession in their home countries. You may find your potential for re-entry has been reduced by a spell overseas. In many professions there used to be a positive attitude to a period of work abroad. It was seen as an attractive addition to one's CV. That is not so common today, at least in the West. Once you have moved out, it becomes increasingly difficult to return. So, more and more, when you opt for service abroad you might be burning your professional bridges.

Here the 'rights' question can raise its head again!

'Don't I have the right to exercise my gifts, training and opportunities to the maximum? Why should God call on me to make this sacrifice?'

God is the only one with real rights! It does us no harm to remind ourselves of that.

> **God is the only one with real rights!**

'You are not your own; you were bought at a price' (1 Corinthians 6:19,20). We shall look at this again in the final chapter. In the self-oriented climate that surrounds us, it can be hard to come to terms with this, but there's no escaping it. And it is wise to settle it in our minds before the testing time comes, so that it takes root in our thinking. As an older Canadian missionary remarked to me, 'It's a Lordship issue.'

It helps us to remember why it is that God calls some people to walk this road. Like Paul (see Romans 1:14,15), we have an obligation. Paul speaks of his being a 'debtor' to the nations, having an obligation to play his part in bringing the gospel of Christ to those who haven't heard. If we don't go, who will? And then how will they hear? So there's a powerful reason to go, powerful enough to outweigh our sacrifices.

This gives a wonderful value to our role. What greater privilege than to play a part in bringing the light of Christ to people for whom he died? How can we really compare that with the best that the world can give? Take all your honours and rewards: what will they matter after a few years? And your acceptance by professional peers? Put that

> **What greater privilege than to bring the light of Christ to people for whom he died?**

alongside the penetrating words of Jesus: 'How can you believe if you accept praise from one another, yet make no effort to obtain the praise that comes from the only God?' (John 5:44).

Let's keep our sacrifices in perspective. They will be real; it would be foolish to pretend otherwise. But Jesus himself promised that we will be generously compensated. 'A hundred times,' he said (Matthew 19:29). The mission field is not full of missionaries bemoaning their lot! Most have already proved the truth of Christ's promise, in one form or another. Christ's service, even when it is costly, is true wealth, not deprivation. Consider the force of Jesus' words in the parable of the rich fool (Luke 12:13–21). The fool is described as 'not rich towards God'. The path the fool has neglected is not really one of poverty but of true riches – of being rich towards God; rich with the character God creates in his children; rich with the joy of fellowship with the living God.

> **Christ's service, even when it is costly, is true wealth, not deprivation.**

Let's see our losses in the light of Paul's consuming ambition:

> *'I consider everything a loss compared to the surpassing greatness of knowing Christ Jesus my Lord, for whose sake I have lost all things. I consider them rubbish, that I may gain Christ and be found in him...I want to know Christ and the power of his*

resurrection and the
fellowship of sharing in his
sufferings, becoming like him
in his death... Not that I have
already obtained all this, or
have already been made
perfect, but I press on to take
hold of that for which Christ
Jesus took hold of me.
Brothers, I do not consider
myself yet to have taken
hold of it. But one thing I do:
Forgetting what is behind
and straining towards what is
ahead, I press on towards the
goal to win the prize for
which God has called me
heavenwards in Christ Jesus.
(Philippians 3:8–14)

CHAPTER 6

Such dangerous places!

S tories like Ruth's and Janet's here are
fortunately very unusual. Their ordeals
were deep personal tragedies. We don't
include them because you will have similar experiences:
you most probably won't. But we include them because
they are true. They are part of the whole picture. Such
things do happen, and they can happen to God's people.

Of course, they happen in our home countries, too.
Every day we read of violence and of crippling and fatal
accidents. To have a balanced view of life and its risks we
need to remember that. But there is no doubt that these
things happen more often in the developing countries. If
you stay at home you can't be sure of escaping accidents,
disease or violence; but if you're called to live in one of
the developing countries you do increase your risks. But, I
say again, remember that these tragic incidents are
unusual; we shouldn't become paralysed by fear.

Ruth Clark's story

We had been in Ethiopia for six years. I was
leaving for a three-day trip as part of my
counselling ministry. With my daughter home
from boarding school, it was a trip I would

have preferred not to make, but because of the special needs in this case I agreed to go. I set out with a pastor, his two young sons and two Ethiopian friends. Our journey was to the town of Jimma, eight hours south of Addis Ababa, where we lived. Two hours from Jimma our Land Cruiser was hit head-on by a truck carrying seven tons of coffee beans. The nine-year-old travelling in the middle of the front seat, so with no safety belt, felt a hand against his chest pushing him back against the seat. The next thing he remembered was seeing me fly over him from the middle of the back seat.

They found me unconscious, between the front and back seats. I had seven broken ribs, my left shoulder blade was broken, and I had a head injury. My back was broken just between my shoulder blades, and my spinal cord damaged. Two of the others had broken arms, but the rest were not seriously hurt.

The mission's medical team reached us four hours later, with pain relief medication and other supplies. I had to spend the night in the wrecked car before a helicopter could fly in the next morning, through a break in the clouds, and fly me out to Addis. Late that afternoon I was flown to Nairobi, Kenya, where specialist care is better. It took twenty-eight hours before I arrived at the hospital.

It took twenty-eight hours before I arrived at the hospital.

Four weeks later, after a long, traumatic flight, I was in Charlotte, USA.

In spite of all the fine medical care that followed, I will be paralysed from my chest down for the rest of my life unless God does a miracle. Our ministry in Ethiopia has ended. I am a paraplegic.

On my first Sunday out of hospital, we were celebrating communion. The pastor explained that the bread represented Jesus' body broken for us, and suddenly a thought hit me and overwhelmed me. It was as if the Lord were saying, 'Ruth, are you willing for your body to be broken for me?' The fact is... it is broken. The question was, 'Are you willing?'

> 'Ruth, are you willing for your body to be broken for me?'

Was I willing? There it was, right in front of me. I had a choice. That choice was not only for the future, but for every minute of every day and every night.

Sometimes if I'm feeling down or in an irritable mood, I'm not the least willing. And I can rationalise lots of reasons why I deserve the right to be down, but it doesn't help! I've needed to work through some heavy issues and I'm not finished yet, but if I take these attitudes and hurts to my Lord when I first realise I'm struggling, it takes a lot less time to work through them.

Sometimes I ask to see his perspective, or at least to have a glimpse of it. Sometimes I ask him to help me focus on things I have to be thankful for in the past. Sometimes I ask him to help me see the humour in situations and be able to laugh. Then sometimes I need him to forgive me for an unkind attitude. Overall, I'm learning to be content, and to be thankful for every day.

> **Overall, I'm learning to be content, and to be thankful for every day.**

Paul tells the Philippians that they have been given the privilege of suffering on behalf of Christ. ('It has been granted to you on behalf of Christ not only to believe on him, but also to suffer for him' Philippians 1:29). I'm still working on the fact that I've been given this wheelchair. My prayer is that through this chair I'll bring glory to God.[6]

Janet Brown's story

A few years ago I read *Joy Unspeakable* by Martyn Lloyd Jones. It left me with questions: 'Is there more to following Jesus than I know?' 'Where is the joy he speaks about, in my life?' 'Am I missing out on something?'

Now as I write, I finally feel that I have made a tiny step forward in knowing God's blessing. There have been some tough moments... Being airlifted out of war-torn Monrovia by US marines. Losing everything – friends, home, ministry, possessions and even a sense of vision for what God wanted to do. Being attacked in our home in Côte d'Ivoire

6. Brian and Ruth Clark served with SIM in Liberia for six years and then in Ethiopia for six years before being attached to the SIM-USA office.

teaches us a similar lesson.
Half of the pieces of
armour he describes are
what the soldier will put on
in the camp before the
battle, not when the
enemy is rushing at him!
With that picture of the

> **We all need to prepare ourselves, mentally and spiritually, for the uncertainties of the future.**

armour as a starter, let's explore what else we should hang
around the gallery of our minds to reflect on.

Not just numbers

We've been using words like 'unusual', 'probably' and
'risk'. Those words have their value, but they shouldn't
make this discussion sound like a statistical exercise. We
are not mere statistics, but children of a heavenly Father,
the one who is on the throne of the universe. If
unwelcome things do happen to us, it's not because we're
merely the victims of probability theory. Thank God for
that! No, they come from the mystery of God's plan, a
plan that flows from his
wisdom, love and power. There
are no accidents for his
children. As Michael Griffiths
said in his address at the
memorial service for the
missionaries killed in a road
accident in Thailand (see below), 'With God there are
mysteries, but no mistakes'.

> **With God there are mysteries, but no mistakes.**

When we hear of disasters in countries which are
known for risk, we often think of those caught up in them
as mere statistics. If we hear floods have made 200,000
people homeless, we may do no more than register a six-
figure number. But each one of those people is the object

of God's love. He is the God who doesn't forget even one sparrow (Luke 12:6). Those thousands are known to God individually. They are people whom he made in his image. But for expatriate Christians who live in those places, the perspective is very different. They identify with their neighbours and those with whom they work; they enjoy friendship with them.

Good out of evil

When we, too, experience difficulties and tragedies, it can have huge effects on how we are perceived by nationals. Some years ago a mission working in Zambia went through an extraordinary series of tragedies in quite a short space of time. This included several deaths in missionary families. The Zambians were used to having missionaries enter into their sorrows and attend their funerals. The missionaries, on the other hand, tended to return to their home countries when they retired. So when they died (usually some years later) they were buried at home, far from those they worked amongst. Now for the first time, the roles were reversed. The Zambians were attending Westerners' funerals, and sharing their griefs. The deepened bonds that grew out of that experience did more for the work than words could express.

So, too, some fruit has been seen from the tragedy in Manorom, Thailand[8]. One warm January day, a minibus full of missionary families from OMF's Manorom Christian Hospital was returning from an outing. A heavy truck coming towards them pulled out in their path from behind a bus, and in the head-on collision that followed five missionaries, seven of their children, and three unborn babies were killed outright. Why did it happen? On the

8. January 1978. The story is retold in *Faith in Tough Places* (OMF/Monarch) by Jan Greenough.

twentieth anniversary of the event, David Pickard, then OMF's General Director, wrote: 'From a less clouded perspective, we can see that God did more that day, and since, than we could have imagined. The Lord promised that we will bear much fruit, and fruit that will last. He never specified how. We have been permitted to see some fruit from the accident in our lifetime. Much will only come to light when we get to heaven.'

> **Much will only come to light when we get to heaven.**

He adds that he has met dozens of men and women, from all over the world, whom God changed through hearing about the accident. An Australian doctor who lost a child in the crash wrote the following month: 'Manorom, which is known as a very hard place in its reaction to the gospel message, has softened in a way that is hardly believable. At a memorial service on the Tuesday after the accident, hundreds of market people and government officials sat and listened intently to the message of hope.'

A New Zealand surgeon on duty that day had waved off his wife and three children in the morning. Only his son survived. On hearing that his wife and daughters had been killed on impact, he had to set about operating on the survivors. He reflected, 'God does not have to justify to me, or give his reasons for, what he has permitted.'

> **'God does not have to justify to me, or give his reasons for, what he has permitted.'**

That is true, and came from a profound acceptance that God is God. Yet in his kindness the Lord does often lift a corner of the curtain to let us see something of the good he plans to bring.

Christ's suffering

Perhaps the biblical theme that can best prepare us for the possibility of hardships is the suffering of Christ. Looking way back into the Old Testament, we find that one of the roles marked out for the Messiah who was to come is that of a servant. It is one of the great themes of the latter part of the book of Isaiah. And if one asks, 'What kind of servant is he?' the answer is clear. He is pre-eminently the suffering servant. 'His appearance was so disfigured beyond that of any man and his form marred beyond human likeness' (Isaiah 52:14). 'A man of sorrows, and familiar with suffering' (Isaiah 53:3). Store this picture in your mind, so that you think of it again when the going gets rough.

That wonderful passage in Isaiah takes it further. It was not just that he suffered, but that his sufferings should have been ours: he takes them in our place. 'He was pierced for our transgressions, he was crushed for our iniquities... The Lord has laid on him the iniquity of us all' (Isaiah 53:5,6). Perhaps we should add that aspect to our mental foundation-laying. We are responsible for that suffering; it is not something we can view objectively; and it is the only basis for our spiritual healing.

The apostle Peter quotes this passage from Isaiah in his first letter, and in the process he gives us one of the Bible's great explanations of Jesus' death (1 Peter 2:21–25). But what is so striking is that he is applying Jesus' death, and Isaiah's predictions of his sufferings, to encourage those who were suffering. At this point he is writing particularly to slaves who were being treated harshly by their masters (verse 18), and we can imagine that that was no picnic! He sympathises with them in their hardships, but urges them to respond with willing service and without retaliation. And to help them in that, he points them to the example of Jesus. So we can put it to the same use, as we need it.

Identifying with Christ in his sufferings

We have seen how, in his suffering, Christ identifies with us and dies in our place. He dies that we might not suffer the ultimate suffering – that of hell. But as Paul thinks about the sufferings of God's people, he builds in this thought: we can identify with Christ in his sufferings! He picks up this theme when he writes to the Colossian Christians: 'I rejoice in what was suffered for you, and I fill up in my flesh what is still lacking in regard to Christ's afflictions, for the sake of his body, which is the Church' (Colossians 1:24). In this difficult passage, Paul is not teaching that he shares in Christ's bearing our sins. Rather, he sees the Church as bearing a burden of suffering in this world. And as the Church

> **He sees the church as bearing a burden of suffering in this world.**

is Christ's body, he sees the Church's suffering as Christ's suffering. Paul counts it a privilege to take his share of that suffering – to contribute towards its completion.

Turning back now to Philippians 3, we feel ourselves responding just as Janet did. We meet in that wonderful passage words which at first we wish Paul had not included. In verse 10 he expresses his highest and deepest aspiration: 'I want to know Christ and the power of his resurrection'. We warm to the challenge of having the same ambition. But then he adds: 'and the fellowship of his sufferings, becoming like him in his death'. Immediately we feel out of our depth. How can we desire that? Perhaps our difficulty is because we haven't seen that the last phrase is inseparable from the first. Elsewhere Paul writes that 'everyone who wants to live a godly life in Christ Jesus will be persecuted' (2 Timothy 3:12). It is suffering for Christ's sake that Paul has in mind, and his words reflect that the more we 'know' Christ, and the more we 'want to live a godly life in Christ Jesus', the more we will want the whole package – including the suffering.

Perhaps this theme, more than most, reinforces Peter's plea to prepare our minds. It would be very hard to apply these things to our circumstances if we started to wrestle with them when the battle is already on and we are facing extreme hardships. We need to be laying these foundations now, building them into the way we think, and then they will come more readily to mind

> **The theme of suffering and glory is an intrinsic part of the gospel.**

when we need them. The theme of suffering and glory is an intrinsic part of the gospel. To change the metaphor again, it is worth setting aside time to mine its rich depths.

Suffering and evangelism

A few years ago Jorge Atiencia, an Ecuadorean who worked amongst students in IFES movements in South America for over thirty years, was expounding 1 Peter to a major European youth missions conference. He noted how the themes of suffering and witness, that is the Christian's response to suffering and its effect on the persecutors, are interwoven in the letter, and he left us with this thought: 'How can our

> **'How can our suffering be an evangelistic tool?'**

suffering be an evangelistic tool?' What a picture to store in our minds! Here is a call not to withdraw from the battle when we are wounded but to see how our hardships could advance the gospel. It happened in the early church. It has happened repeatedly through the history of the church. It is happening today.

We turn to the Manorom tragedy again for a striking example. Adèle Juzi's five-year-old son, Lukas, had been on the outing. She jumped into her car as soon as she heard of the accident, and drove to the scene. There she learned of the death of the twelve, who included Lukas. She writes:

'As I looked at the Thai people gathered round, my heart was filled with pity for them. I prayed, and turning to them I said, "These people who have died are not here any more. They are already with the Lord, and they were ready to meet him. I have one wish – that you, all of you, will never forget this sad scene, and that whenever you hear anything about the Lord Jesus you will open your hearts to him, so that when you too have to die you will be as ready to meet the Lord as these people have been."'

The fruit of the Spirit is ... joy

Again and again, when you meet Christians who have suffered severely, the difference between the Christian life and stoicism stands out.

There is no situation in which the Spirit cannot produce his fruit, and part of that fruit is joy. Incredible though it may seem to others, Christians can know joy even in suffering. Perhaps not easily, but really.

> **Christians can know joy even in suffering. Perhaps not easily, but really.**

I recall hearing the following account of one woman's experience. Soon after she became a Christian, there began a period when she moved from one tragedy or hardship to another, in her own life or her family's. The whole story was so grim one could have forgiven her for thinking God had forsaken her. But as she recounted the story, her final words were, 'The wonderful thing is that in all this God never let me down!' Janet and David and Brian and Ruth would say the same. They have proved God in painful and exacting experiences. They need to be heard.

I close this chapter with a quote from Joni Eareckson-Tada. She was paralysed from the neck downwards in a diving accident while still at high school. This intelligent, athletic, artistic teenager suddenly found herself in a wheelchair for the rest of her life. She, like Ruth, has come to terms with the fact that God has given her this wheelchair. In a Foreword to a book on healing she reflects:

'I have been in a wheelchair now for over three decades, and, thankfully, have found a deeper healing that satisfies: profound peace, a settled soul, strengthened faith, and a lively, buoyant hope of heaven.'[9]

> 'I have found a deeper healing that satisfies, and a buoyant hope of heaven.'

9. Joni Eareckson-Tada, *Miraculous Healing* (Christian Focus/OMF). She has written a range of books which speak into situations of suffering, and which turn readers' eyes towards the hope of what is unseen.

CHAPTER 7

Marriage, family life and singleness

L et's look at two different situations, world's away from the West.

Sarah's story

Sarah is an Interserve partner. (Her name has been changed as she works in a sensitive area.)

Sarah works in central Asia among the Tibetan Buddhists, a group that few people know much about. She had hoped other Christians from her country might join her, but nobody did, so she went alone. She has made her home in a village on the edge of the grasslands where nomads roam, and she is the only foreigner in the area. It is a four-hour journey by bus from any other English-speaking people, and from any Christian fellowship.

She teaches in a school with around 60 children and five other staff, one of whom gets drunk regularly. The cook's husband beats the children, as does one of the teachers if they don't learn fast enough. A lonely woman leans on her for support and friendship, and makes demands on her when her energy is gone and she is weary.

The school day starts at 6.00 a.m. with physical exercises. She doesn't need to take part, but daily living is time-consuming, and this is the cue to light the burner to cook breakfast. The cow dung eventually smoulders into flame. If it is in short supply, sheep manure has to be used instead, which isn't nearly so effective, and can easily slip through the grate.

The school is meant to have a supply of electricity in the evening, but this is erratic. A nearby spring supplies freezing cold water for washing and drinking. It's hardly surprising that none of the children or staff wash either their clothes or themselves for months at a time; nor that the children's hair is infested with lice.

The school supply of electricity is erratic.

By 7.00 a.m. students call at her door for help with their lessons. Then she teaches a class, and after that a stream of staff and other visitors come and go. Every day is the same, with no privacy, from 7.00 a.m. to 10.00 p.m. with no rest. Students and staff all live on the school grounds, which are barely bigger than a football pitch.

Sarah asks her friends to pray for her attitudes. In such a small community, the adults pass their time in gossip and criticism. How can she keep out of it? She finds herself being resentful that her time and her possessions are all public property.

Christians working in the nearest city go out to visit Sarah as often as they can, and take her fresh vegetables to augment her diet. She still hopes others may come to join her in her ministry some time. It's a long-term work and a costly one. Sarah moved thousands of miles away from her family and her boyfriend to settle among these people, and bring them, in the words of the apostle Paul, 'the sweet savour of Christ'. As with others in this book, she felt the love of Christ left her no choice.

Andrew and Jean's story

Andrew and Jean are part of a team working for Mongolia's development. This letter came shortly after they reached their new home. The climate is inhospitable; temperatures range from –40C to +40C.

After two long months our crate finally arrived. No Christmas boxes have ever been so exciting. Now we have all the clothes, bedding and other items we need to cope with a Mongolian winter. Our petrol stove and tilley lamp have proved invaluable, but fuel is extremely hard to come by.

We began our time here with no electricity, an erratic water supply, and no heating. We are grateful that the Language Institute we work with has provided us with a small generator that can power the twin-tub washing machine. We now have a fairly regular water supply and heating. Today we also had hot water for the first time. Wonderful!

We are stocking up for the winter, now that

our balcony can double up as a freezer. Last week Andrew came back from market with a 21kg leg of beef on his back. We then spent the evening butchering it on our living room table. It cost about 15p per pound. We are becoming increasingly carnivorous as vegetables have all but disappeared from the shops.

Language lessons have been enjoyable, although we struggle to find time to study. We learned a valuable lesson in pronunciation a while ago – for the first month we'd been proudly announcing in Mongolian that we were 'British birds' rather than 'British people'. This probably explains the puzzled reactions.

Andrew is enjoying the Excel correspondence course for Mongolian English teachers. To help overcome the lack of speaking practice, four-day seminars are held every few months. In addition to this we have started an 'English Club', which meets every week. It helps us to get to know the students and gives them language practice, as well as being good fun. One student, PJ, asked for a copy of our 'favourite book'. Jean has also begun teaching English in a nearby primary school for 40 minutes a day.

Our first visit to a *ger* (a Mongolian tent) was an interesting experience. It is a Mongolian tradition to present first-time visitors with large mounds of *buudz* (greasy meat pies) and salty tea. One-year-old Thomas wolfed them down with great relish. However, Andrew, suffering from sickness the previous day, had to force down every mouthful, and only just made it home in time! We continue to meet weekly in the *ger* to look at Mark's Gospel, which is a great joy and privilege.

Towards the end of last month, Rose (three years old) fell off a seat onto the hard floorboards and broke her collarbone. Fortunately Jean, who has broken her collarbone twice before, knew what to do. After three weeks she is mending well. She continues to be our extrovert toddler and last week ran up to a little gaggle of children in the post office and asked them to be her friends. Although they didn't understand her, they proceeded to follow her home. We continue to have a trail of children coming to play. Thomas is well and speaks as much Mongolian as he does English!

We continue to have a trail of children coming to play.

With love and best wishes
Andrew and Jean

For some people, life does not include marriage. And that group is especially significant in the world of mission. But single and married missionaries alike need to make their host country their home country, and to feel at home in their house, apartment or *ger*. So what are some of the costs, for home life, of obeying a call to serve abroad? Let's look first at singleness.

Marriage was God's creation, and is given some prominence from the very beginning. See how the first two chapters of Genesis, which bring out different aspects of creation, both put the spotlight on the creation of the sexes, and their relationships and roles. And when the story begins a downward spiral, in chapter 3, it is again the relationship of the man and the woman that is highlighted.

Marriage is the norm for the human race. It is a gift from God. Most people choose marriage, and many single people are not single by choice. So, if I am single, but would still prefer to be married, how will that be affected by a call to serve God abroad? Most people going abroad long-term have reached their late twenties or early thirties before they go. So, even if they stay at home, the prospects of marriage are, humanly speaking, reduced by that stage.

And how does a move to life in another culture affect the situation? Even in cities the number of compatible people you will meet is almost certainly less than you would meet at home. We find examples of people who have met their life partner while at Bible College or after they arrived in their host country, but they are a minority. So comes the question for the single person: granted that God has made you with a desire for marriage, do you have a right to maximise your chances, to avoid taking a route that is likely to reduce them?

How does a move to life in another culture affect the situation?

Marriage and singleness – both are gifts

It's time to look again at the biblical perspective on this. We saw above that marriage is a gift. So those who are married should see their marriage as something God has given them. That could lead us to think of singleness as a state of deprivation, and singles as those from whom God has withheld a blessing. Let's turn to 1 Corinthians 7, and discover how Paul sees it. In this long and complicated chapter Paul gives us teaching relating to marriage and singleness. Some of it is difficult to interpret with confidence, and certain verses may have particular application to the Corinthians' circumstances at the time. But some parts are very clear.

So, for example, in verse 7 Paul writes: 'I wish that all men were as I am'. By that he means 'unmarried'. Then he continues: 'But each man has his own gift from God; one has this gift, another has that.' Clearly he sees our state – whether married or single – as something God has given us. So singleness, too, is a positive gift and not a condition of deprivation. This reflects the Bible's consistent picture of God as both heavenly Father and sovereign Lord. Our lives aren't the product of our own choices operating within a world of blind chance. God shapes all the facets of our lives, through his power, wisdom and love. We can sympathise with the person who responded to the idea of singleness as a gift from God with the comment: 'The gift that nobody wants!' It may at times seem an unwelcome gift, but it is a gift from a loving Father.

There's another biblical insight into singleness, in the words of Jesus in Matthew 19:3–12. Jesus is teaching about the sanctity of marriage. His high standards prompt the retort from his disciples that if divorce is as hard to get as Jesus was teaching, it might be better not to get married in the first place! Jesus responds by saying that not everyone is called to singleness. But he identifies some groups of people who do remain single. Amongst these he describes those who 'have renounced marriage because of the kingdom of heaven' (verse 12). We have pointed out that many single people would prefer to be married. But Jesus identifies another group, whose singleness is voluntary – for the sake of greater usefulness to God. God may call only a few down that path, but we shouldn't overlook the fact that he does call some.

If we are to see both marriage and singleness as gifts from God, then we should expect to see each state as having its own advantages and disadvantages. We might also expect that each would show particular advantages and particular drawbacks when transplanted into another culture.

We've already mentioned the disadvantage for singles in going overseas that this reduces the likelihood of finding a husband or wife. Singleness can be a lonely business, especially when you encounter all sorts of new situations. It is a help to have someone to talk them through with.

> **Singleness can be a lonely business.**

An unfamiliar culture can throw up all sorts of tensions for a single person. Many of the cultures in developing countries have more restrictive ideas of acceptable behaviour for single people than we are used to in the comparatively free and easy cultures in the West. They won't just be different; sometimes they will be irritatingly rigid! And to ignore them will, in many cases, destroy our usefulness. Using our homes for entertainment can be more difficult. A married couple can easily invite visitors of either sex. The single person won't be free to entertain singles of the opposite sex in

> **An unfamiliar culture can throw up all sorts of tensions for a single person.**

their home. Likewise, there will be some pastoral tasks that a single person can't undertake.

Housing, opportunities, friendships

Many agencies working abroad own housing for their workers. It may be a financially sensible arrangement but sometimes it produces friction. This can be true for anyone, but mission housing can be particularly difficult for singles. They are often allocated a house, and may have little or no choice as to whom they share the house with. After all, married couples have had the choice of whom they are to live with – for the rest of their lives. But the single person may have to share a house with a missionary colleague with whom they have little natural affinity and wouldn't choose to spend a holiday with, let alone a four-year term. But there may be no option, other than to return home, defeated. The only route is for us to accept the situation with good grace. In that process many people have been surprised to discover some wonderful lasting friendships.

There are significant advantages to being single, however. In 1 Corinthians 7, Paul points out that married people have all sorts of distracting cares. Single people have only themselves. This gives them greater freedom and flexibility, for example in the use of their time and energy. It is no surprise, then, that some single people have found themselves in fruitful activities that would be impossible for a married man or woman. I think

> **Some single people have found themselves in fruitful activities that would be impossible for a married man or woman.**

of Gerry, for example, working amongst nomadic peoples, in a ministry which calls for him to spend a lot of his time on the move, to keep in touch with the people he is trying to reach. Or take the story of Sarah at the beginning of this chapter. We could multiply examples. Not all would be as extreme. Some simply show that a single person can sometimes give themselves to a task with less distraction, and fruit can flow from that.

> **There is a richness in the range of pure friendships that a single person can enjoy.**

The friendships that are open to the single person are also a plus. It is sad that today's confused moral values in the West mean there is a danger that people will suspect all same-sex friendships of being lesbian or gay. We need to be alert to that. But there is a richness in the range of pure friendships that a single person can enjoy.

Family life

The family life of married couples, too, is affected by being suddenly transported into the setting of a foreign culture. Some of the costs have been touched on in other chapters, and the next chapter looks particularly at the costs for our children.

The Christian home and family is a place where outsiders should be welcomed and find blessing. It is not surprising that one of the qualifications for spiritual leaders in the New Testament churches is hospitality. But the family also needs time when they are together, when the

> **The family also needs time when they are together.**

MISSIONARIES' PARENTS
(For short-termers and long-termers)

In Chapter 8 we touch on missionaries' responsibilities for their children – and the tremendous privileges those children have of growing up in a Christian home. Here we look briefly at missionaries' responsibilities to their parents. We have read of Jason (page 16), whose father at first showed hostility to his son's plans to go to the Muslim world. Later Jason saw his father's attitude soften. If we were closer to the two, we would see the parts played by their personalities, their convictions and their cultures. Yes, their cultures, too. In these days of rapidly-changing cultures in the West and East, we need to understand the culture factor among the mix of factors which contribute to conflict and to subsequent harmony.

This was obviously a painful episode in the relationship between father and son. In countries of rapid change the differences of age and changing culture can be a cause of severe tension. This is especially true where some family members have relocated to the West from Asian or African contexts. The younger generation is westernised but the older generation retains Asian or African values. For in many East Asian and African cultures we still find a respect which leads to real differences being suppressed.

Parting from families is always painful. It can be all the more so when parents have not understood or accepted their children's decision to live in a foreign culture. That may be because they want to see their grandchildren grow up – a very natural desire. Or perhaps they genuinely fear their children are making a bad decision and should be using their education to 'a better advantage'. It may be because they have personal concerns for health or financial security, and feel they need their family's support to be nearer to hand.

It is good to remember that our parents know us better than we sometimes think. Even if they don't share our Christian convictions, they have imbibed much of who we are from seeing us as young children, and through our rebellions, whatever form those took. If they are wise and perceptive people, whether Christians or not, they will have advice which is good to hear, and to consider carefully.

There may be good reason for staying at home a little longer to care for parents or other relatives, if you are best placed to do that. Katherine Porter made this decision (page 65, 66). If your parents are in difficulties financially, it would be right and good to ensure before you go that their needs will be met. These are issues which need to be discussed openly with brothers or sisters, or with other members of the wider family.

It is good and biblical to consider our parents' needs. As you talk through your sense of call with your church leaders, include this very important aspect. To leave with your parents' blessing is blessing indeed. There will be families where that cannot happen. If that is your situation, put in every effort to rebuild trust through keeping in close contact, asking their advice, sharing personal news. That in itself will count for more than you know.

special bonds that we find in families are refreshed and strengthened. Children need time with parents; husbands and wives need time for and from each other. In our home cultures these things are taken for granted and, if they don't happen, it is in most cases our own fault. Our society leaves us alone. But in many other cultures it is very hard to find ways of shutting the rest of society out of the home for a while. Privacy seems impossible to find. At these times we find ourselves protesting – perhaps only in our own minds – that we are entitled to better than that. We want to claim the right to privacy, but we may have to adapt to the culture and accept that we will have less privacy than we would like. This, too, may be a price we have to pay.

We may have to accept that we will have less privacy.

For some parents a major cost lies in exposing themselves and their children to harsh and primitive conditions. Our God-given instinct is to protect our children; it goes deeply against the grain to bring them into hardship. Andrew and Jean, whose story is here, must have felt that keenly when they sensed the Lord calling them to work in Mongolia. At their valedictory service in the UK, both described something of how they sensed God's call. Andrew added that, from the time they were engaged, they began to pray for children who would not only survive, but thrive, in tough conditions. Their commitment to that prayer has been amply tested!

They began to pray for children who would not only survive, but thrive.

God's companionship

What do we say to all this? I want to pick out just two biblical themes. First, to those who struggle with loneliness in singleness, the Bible presents us with a Father who is concerned for our needs and can help us in them. So in Psalm 145 David celebrates a God who is our creator, and 'loving towards all he has made' (verses 13,17). We think readily enough of God's wisdom and power being displayed in creation, but the Bible links it with God's compassion and love. Apply this not to people in general, but to yourself, as his beloved child.

In Psalm 146:9, as in other passages, his concern is focused not on the mass of humanity, but on the isolated in particular. He is the God who sustains the fatherless and the widow. And we may surely add 'and the single'. This isn't trivialising the normal role of father or husband but, rather, it asserts that the help and support that God can give are very real. Remember, he is our Creator, and he knows how to help, as no one else could ever do.

We find this balanced recognition of the natural ways of support and God's ability to replace them in Paul's experience towards the end of his life. In 2 Timothy 4:16 he reveals how much he felt the need of friends to support him, and how deserted he felt when they were not there: 'At my first defence, no-one came to my support, but everyone deserted me'. We sense a note of wistfulness. Here is no super-spiritual denial of his need for human comfort. Then he goes on to say: 'But the Lord stood at my side and gave me strength'. The absence of human friends was a real loss, but God's help was even more real.

The longing for privacy

And then, to those who chafe at not having a 'proper' home, and who find the loss of privacy hard to take and the intrusion of strangers irksome, let me bring two examples from the life and words of the Lord Jesus Christ. The first is his description of the lifestyle he chose for himself: 'Foxes have holes and birds of the air have nests, but the Son of Man has nowhere to lay his head' (Matthew 8:20). That's a pretty vulnerable lifestyle.

The second example is in his attitude to people – people who could be such a demanding nuisance. Remember how they even pursued him across the lake, when he was looking for a bit of peace and quiet with his friends (Matthew 14:13–15). Matthew records his response on another occasion: 'When he saw the crowds he had compassion on them, because they were harassed and helpless, like sheep without a shepherd' (Matthew 9:36). He is a hard act to follow. But that is what he calls us to. And where he calls, he also gives the needed grace.

CHAPTER 8

What do we owe our children?

Christian parents probably shed more tears and have deeper feelings of failure over their families than over anything else. Children give their parents so much joy, and there is every reason to thank God for them. Yet the task of bringing them up exposes our weaknesses and gives plenty of scope for our sinfulness to find expression.

The family life of people in so-called 'full-time Christian ministry' presents some special problems. That applies to those working in their own culture as well as to those working abroad. And this is especially true for those whose work is partly or largely done from home. There the balance between the demands of ministry and the demands of children becomes particularly hard to get right.

> **Our temperaments will tend to push us to one extreme or the other.**

Our temperaments will tend to push us to one extreme or the other. The activist, with very high commitment to the ministry, will be inclined to respond instantly to the call of the work, and leave family responsibilities neglected or even

117

unnoticed. That's a sure formula for creating resentment in the wife or husband, and in the children. No surprise if the children even come to resent their parents' faith which – as they see it – is responsible for their neglect. And they may then struggle with inappropriate guilt over that resentment.

Then there's the opposite extreme. We can become so protective of our family and time with them – especially if we are working abroad – that people might well wonder why we are there at all. And our supporters might have the same question! If our sole aim is to care for our family and spend time with our children, we could, after all, do that at home.

Fashions of thinking amongst Christians can swing from one of these extremes to the other. So it's good to know ourselves, and also to recognise what fashion is currently in force!

'Third-culture' children

This is the new term for what used to be called 'missionary kids' or 'MKs'. It's a good one, because children growing up in a host culture, and not the culture of their parents, end up able to live happily in both cultures without feeling that they really belong fully to either. Theirs is a 'third culture'. And there are problems here, as well as privileges.

There always will be problems and dangers for families in this fallen world. There is no escaping them, as we all know from our own childhood. But bringing up a family in a foreign culture brings its own share of difficulties.

Let's look at four different scenes:

[Scene 1] Somewhere in Africa
Little Tim, four years of age, is the oldest child of an Asian father and a British mother – missionaries. Until he goes to

school, his only companions are the children of the local church leader. The child closest to Tim in age is an aggressive little boy, and untruthful. Tim learns to lie, too.

His parents are in a dilemma. They know Tim needs other children to play with, but in their home countries he would have the chance to choose his friends. To withdraw him from the company of these children would give him a solitary existence, and carry the real risk of offending the church leader and his wife!

At last it is time for Tim to go to school. Surely this will solve the problems. He is sent to a school for expatriate children in the nearby city. The fees are high, but his parents believe it is worth it. However, there are different problems now.

The school is not primarily for missionary children; most of the pupils are from wealthy expatriate families, enjoying a lifestyle far above that of Tim and his parents. When birthday parties come round, Tim inevitably compares what he sees when he goes to the birthday parties of his new friends with what his parents can manage. That is not easy for Tim or his parents to handle. It obviously troubles him.

After a while the teachers call Tim's parents in and explain that they are concerned about him. He is becoming withdrawn and antisocial. They recommend he be taken to a child psychiatrist. Six months later, things are looking brighter. Tim is happier, and relating better to his peers. That crisis is over.

But life would have been simpler if they had stayed in the UK!

[Scene 2] In Central Asia

Carl and Liz are working in a Central Asian country. The culture has been hardened by decades of harsh totalitarian government. One ugly feature of this is the use of 'shaming' or public humiliation as the normal means of offering correction or reproof – for example in the workplace. This is something of a shock compared with Western (especially North American) cultures, where the prevailing view is that people respond better to encouragement. Carl and Liz manage to cope with this themselves, but find it very difficult to think of their children having to do so. And it is the primary motivating 'tool' used by the teachers at the school where their two sons attend.

[Scene 3] Somewhere in Asia

James moved out to Asia as a toddler, with his British missionary parents. When he reached school age, they were living in a remote village far away from schools, so his mother began home-schooling. Like Tim, above, James' only companions were local children. He quickly picked up their language, and got on well with them. Then friends visiting the home noticed that his behaviour was not developing normally. The cultural gulf between him and his local friends was hampering him. Reluctantly and anxiously, and totally in conflict with what they had planned for their children, his parents accepted that he should go off to the school for missionary children in a neighbouring country.

They shed tears at the parting, but James seemed happy enough, and early reports from the school confirmed that he was well settled. When he came home for the holidays his parents were surprised and delighted at his maturity. When, later, the family returned to the UK for home assignment, relatives remarked on how well he had developed.

Then comes the news that the school at which James

had been so happy will be closing. There is no equivalent possibility. His parents feel perplexed as to what to do. They do not want him, or his younger brothers, to be disadvantaged in their education by their parents' missionary call. All over again, James' parents find themselves facing the battle of 'rights' which they thought was behind them when they joined the mission. Is it not their 'right' to give their children the education of their choice? What are their 'rights' in this situation?

[Scene 4] In the UK

In a public meeting, a young man is describing his experiences as a child of missionaries in Asia, with less money than they would have had at home, disrupted schooling, and all the other things that go with 'third-culture' children's lives.

His uncle had been listening. His own children had received the best education in the UK that money could buy. At the end of the meeting the uncle remarked that their upbringing had been comparatively deprived, alongside the description his nephew had given of his own childhood! There was the enrichment of travel and of different cultures; firm friendships with children from several nationalities; dorm parents who had put him and his fellow students first, who had helped them with their homework, been there at the football games, and encouraged them in their spiritual lives too. And because he was away at school, his parents had made sure there were special times with his family in the holidays. One thing he had never felt in any way was deprived.

* * *

There are real costs to being a 'third-culture' child. Little Tim's problems may not be unusual. Our Western preoccupation with the nuclear family can lead us to

> **Most human societies make good use of the extended family.**

overlook the fact that most human societies make good use of the extended family. Even in our own cultures the extended family plays a more important role than we often realise. So losing that network when we go abroad may be more of a loss than we see at first. Of course, as we make friends in our host country we may find some replacement 'extended family' among them. Now that would be enriching to the whole family!

For the first five years of our first child's life, my wife and I lived in a country far from our families, though in a culture which had much in common with our own. We were struck by our daughter's awareness of the fact that her little friends knew their grandparents, uncles and aunts, cousins, while in her case they were no more than names and photographs. How much more significant it is, then, when a child grows up in a very different culture without their extended family.

But let's remember that the best of parenting and the most privileged and sheltered circumstances can never guarantee that a child will 'turn out all right'. Our children share the same fallen humanity that we do, and only God's grace can prevent them making shipwrecks of their lives. So avoiding a call

> **Our children share the same fallen humanity that we do.**

to serve in another culture won't guarantee a happy or successful family.

As throughout this book, we want to be realistic about the costs of going abroad. So let's look at some of the problem areas. But as we do so, let us not overlook the compensations and advantages. I hope we'll see both sides.

Education

The problems of schooling must rank high in importance for any parent bringing up children in a foreign country. People living in a city in a 'developed' country may find the facilities so good, and so accessible, that they are not conscious of any drawbacks. But things can be very different in less developed areas. Many missionaries are a long way from a school of any description, and cut off from other expatriate families.

Most people today are fortunate in having a choice of several options for their children. Each of these has its passionate devotees who are sometimes dismissive of all other methods. Often, some painful experience brings us to see that the issues are not as clear-cut as we thought, and we are thankful to have access to an option we had previously dismissed. Sometimes the best use of gifts or resources, or the interests of the mission, can point to an option that would not be our first choice.

Take, for example, a situation where there are two families in the same village. One family prefers home schooling, which would be carried out by the mother. The other family would rather have a trained teacher provided, so that the parents can both give more time to mission activities. That teacher could easily handle teaching the children from both families, and the mission leaders see that that would be the best use of resources. What should the first family do? How do 'rights' come into this?

So whatever our own views are, it's best to avoid dogmatism. In particular it's unwise to ascribe any particular family's problem to their views on children's education. Issues, personalities and circumstances in the real world are too complex for that. We may have all the right theories and practices,

> **Whatever our own views are, it's best to avoid dogmatism.**

but we will still be vulnerable, in this area as we are in others. As the apostle Paul cautions us, 'If you think you are standing firm, be careful that you don't fall!' (1 Corinthians 10:12)

Social development

Both Tim and James are examples of children struggling in their social development as they grow up in a foreign culture. Sometimes the effects are less obvious and less serious. Some problems disappear rapidly when the child returns to more familiar circumstances; for other children the effects go deeper.

We need a sense of perspective about this, as on other points. Many children in our home countries suffer in their childhood development. Through tension in the home, bullying at school or from many other causes, children suffer and are damaged. As we have noted already, the problems are not limited to those who live abroad. And the quality of home life is of supreme importance for our children's wellbeing, wherever we may be living. Many 'third-culture' children thrive on their childhood circumstances and develop and mature through them.

> **The quality of home life is of supreme importance.**

Health and safety

In the minds of many people in the West, accidents and disease form part of the general picture of developing countries. And, as we saw in an earlier chapter, that image is not without foundation. Missionaries' children do die of malaria. Some are killed in car accidents. Although children die of disease and accidents in our home countries, the risks are greater in developing countries.

On the other hand, life in many of these places is healthier than we imagine. I remember interviewing a young couple who believed they were called to work in Africa. I noted how the wife abhorred spiders, and observed her almost pathological concern for the cleanliness of their little toddler! I said to myself they would never make it. However, they were convinced of God's call. And I was wrong. My next mental image of them is from a visit I made to the family two years later. Their daughter, now running around, appeared to spend more time eating with the neighbouring African family than with her own, as they all sat on the ground around their communal cooking pot. Her mother was quite unconcerned. And the child was a picture of robust good health! The point is that we so easily get these things out of perspective. Yes, there are degrees of risk, but they are just that: they are degrees; they are relative.

> **Their daughter appeared to spend more time eating with the neighbouring African family.**

* * *

So where is our responsibility in these things? Should we above all else protect our children in a safe environment, and give them the best education? If this is our conclusion, then we should stay at home. Yet we are ignoring the gospel reasons for going. And we are also ignoring the fact that there is no sure way of avoiding all risk while we are in this world. On top of this, we are discounting the significant benefits that our children can gain through the experience.

What had kept James' parents from coming home when their anxieties about his progress, and other hardships, were at their greatest? I asked them. His father thought for a moment. 'We've always been absolutely sure that God had called us to serve abroad,' he replied, 'and I didn't want to be looking back in thirty years' time, regretting what might have been.'

The compensations

The third and fourth scenes at the beginning of this chapter remind us that there is something else to put in the scales as we weigh up the costs. There are many compensations. Most missionary children find themselves greatly enriched by their upbringing. They experience strange places and cultures; they meet people of many nationalities; they learn other languages; they are enriched by the friendship and example of Christian workers they meet.

> **Most missionary children find themselves greatly enriched by their upbringing.**

Of course, there are casualties, as there are amongst children growing up in their parents' home cultures. But most will be the richer for their experiences. The mission community as a whole shows immense concern for the welfare of our children, and invests a vast amount in research into the issue and providing resources to meet their needs. One survey showed that most 'third-culture' children wouldn't hesitate to expose their own children to the upbringing which they themselves had experienced.[10]

Being a Christian parent

Whole books are written on this, of course, and a few paragraphs can't cover the subject. But we have referred to the importance of home life in supporting our children through difficult times, and we should go back to that.

The experience of Carl and Liz and their family (Scene 2) underlines how important loving support is to our children when we are in a strange culture. Carl and Liz need to be countering the corrosive effects of that 'shaming' by unmistakable love and acceptance in the home. Even in less extreme circumstances, children are sustained by the confidence they have in their parents' love and acceptance.

> **Children are sustained by the confidence they have in their parents' love and acceptance.**

A missionary wife and mother wrote this while looking back on her own experience in a boarding school for MKs:

> It wasn't until my final year as a senior that I realised what a special heritage I had. I felt

---

10. See M H Taylor, "Personality Development in the Children of Missionary Parents" in *Helping Missionaries Grow: Readings in Mental Health and Development* (William Carey Library, Pasadena).

close to my parents and knew we had a good, honest relationship, but I took it for granted. It wasn't until one of my classmates opened my eyes to what others felt about the relationship they had with their parents that I understood how fortunate I was. 'Marilyn, your parents really love you, don't they?' my friend asked me one day in one of her more pensive moments. 'Sure they do,' I replied, wondering why she even bothered to bring up the subject. 'Well, I don't think mine love me as much,' she said quietly.[11]

Wise parental love will be sensitive to the differences that can exist between children in the same family. The same missionary describes how she thrived on life in a MK school but her younger sister went through a deep crisis. Their parents needed to be alert to the fact that the two sisters had different personalities and different needs.

Let's turn now to just a few of the biblical guidelines for parents. In Ephesians 6 Paul gives his familiar instruction to fathers to bring their children up 'in the training and instruction of the Lord'. But he adds the thought-provoking command not to 'exasperate' their children! Perhaps parents need to reflect on ways in which they might be 'exasperating' their children. John Stott expounds that word as making irritating or unreasonable demands, showing harshness and cruelty, humiliating or suppressing them, or showing sarcasm and ridicule.[12] In the parallel passage in Colossians 3, Paul urges fathers, 'Do not embitter your children, or they will become discouraged.'

---

11. Marilyn Schlitt, *Deprived or Privileged?* (OMF), p 48.
12. John Stott, *The Message of Ephesians* (IVP), p 246.

In 1 Thessalonians 2, Paul describes his relationship to the Thessalonian believers as 'like a mother' (verse 7) and 'like a father' (verse 11). In so doing he shows us what he thinks mothers and fathers should be like. So the mother is 'gentle…caring for her little children'. The father, in turn, is described as 'encouraging, comforting'.

In all of these passages Paul outlines for us a parental character which would support our children through all kinds of hardships. Many missionaries are natural leaders, and those who lead instinctively may need to take special note of this. Their strength of character can often bypass the gentle encouragement that a child may be urgently needing.

The grace of God

Parents have a deep desire to protect their children and do what is best for them. And we can be very sensitive to the accusation that we are requiring sacrifice of our children for the sake of our own call.

Let's close the chapter with two thoughts about the character of God. First, our God acts graciously – with mercy and compassion. He created parenthood and the family: they are his idea. He is the God who created parental love: he understands it better than we do. So when he calls us to a path that may include some hardship not only for us but for our children, he does it as that kind of God: our gracious Father.

> **Our God acts graciously – with mercy and compassion.**

And the second thought is this: God's grace is undeserved. Whatever he calls us to, and whatever he brings into our lives, the good is more than we deserve,

Education options
• National/local school in host country
• International day school (where available)
• Christian boarding school in host/neighbouring country
• Home schooling
• Boarding school in home country
• Day school in home country (children living with gurardians).

and the hardships are less. In his books the balance is always heavily on that side. He is no man's debtor. As the old hymn has it: 'he giveth and giveth and giveth again.'

CHAPTER 9

Christ with us

We've nearly done. It's time to reflect, and draw this part of the book to a close. We've looked at some of the implications of responding to a call to serve God abroad. Along the way we've reminded ourselves of the overall reasons for going – to bring the gospel to a world that desperately needs to hear it. We've seen there are some real costs and real rewards. We've learned from the experiences of those already there. In this last

> **There are some real costs and real rewards.**

chapter we'll spend a little more time going over some of the biblical themes that can help us in the stock-taking, cost-counting process. We'll choose four that focus on Christ. The first two present us with a high call; the second two lead us to ways in which God gently helps us to respond to that call.

The Lord to be obeyed

People of our generation assert their autonomy. They are their own people, and resent authority. This way of thinking is part of the air we breathe in our Western cultures, and it can seep into our attitudes. It can touch even our relationship with God. Our God is Lord and King! Yes, he is kind and compassionate. Yes, he is gracious and forgiving. But he is also Lord! And Christ shares that lordship. The corollary of that is, as Paul puts it: 'You are not your own; you were bought at a price' – the price of Christ's death for us (1 Corinthians 6:19,20). Jesus is Lord. He is our king. He has absolute right to plan and shape our lives,

> **He has absolute right to plan and shape our lives.**

because we belong to him. We are his because he made us, and his because he bought us.

Earlier in the book we looked at one biblical picture of this – that of the potter. Listen to the words of Isaiah 45: 'Woe to him who quarrels with his Maker, to him who is but a potsherd among the potsherds on the ground. Does the clay say to the potter, "What are you making?"' (verse 9). As he calls us to follow him, Jesus tells us that his yoke is easy (Matthew 11:30). The whole passage (verses 28–30) is full of gentle encouragement. But note that Jesus doesn't say that there is no yoke! There is still a yoke, and a yoke serves to guide the ox where the farmer wants him to go! We

> **We are to be at his disposal, and to go where he directs.**

are to be at his disposal, and to go where he directs. But that bondage is true freedom; that death is true life.

The example to be followed

Examples are there to be followed. An example does two things. It shows that something can be done; it takes an action from the realm of theory into the world of practice. And an example also shows us how it can be done. Jesus is a model for us in both of these ways. So when he calls us to any path of costly obedience, we know this: he is not sending us on some impossible journey, far removed from our world. No, he has walked that path himself. And as we watch him, through the pages of the Bible, we can see how to walk that path ourselves.

One of the most wonderful biblical pictures of Jesus as the 'servant-king' is found in Philippians 2:6–8.

> *...Christ Jesus: Who, being in very nature God, did not consider equality with God something to be grasped, but made himself nothing, taking the very nature of a servant, being made in human likeness. And being found in appearance as a man, he humbled himself and became obedient to death – even death on a cross!*

He was not compelled to come. He had a full right to hold on to all the expressions of his deity. He could have stayed in heaven and avoided all the many features of humanity that were part of his becoming man. But he did not consider that 'something to be grasped'; he surrendered it for us. And Paul brings us these thoughts not only as profound theology, but also quite explicitly as an example for us to follow.

'Your attitude should be the same as that of Christ Jesus.'

Note how he begins this section: 'Your attitude should be the same as that of Christ Jesus.'

The companion who strengthens us

At the end of Matthew's gospel, we find what we often call the 'Great Commission' (Matthew 28:18–20). We opened this book with a quotation from those verses, and the title of this book comes from them. Here Jesus bids his apostles farewell and sends them off on their life's work. As part of that he gives them this promise: 'Surely I am with you always, to the very end of the age.' I think we can easily miss what a profound thing this is. It can seem almost trivial. So it is striking that that simple promise accompanies the great things they are taught ('all authority is given to me') and the great things they are to be doing (preaching, teaching, baptising).

One of the effects of suffering and hardship is to make us feel isolated. Peter recognises this when he tells suffering Christians that their sufferings are the same as those being experienced by others (1 Peter 5:9). It should be a great comfort and encouragement to know that we are never alone. Christ is with us. Two incidents in the life of Paul give us examples of this. During his first missionary travels in Greece, his message was largely rejected in Athens and also (to begin with) in Corinth, the next place on his route. Then one night, in Corinth, the Lord spoke to him in a vision: 'Do not be afraid; keep on speaking, do not be silent. For I am with you' (Acts 18:9,10). That was the answer to his fears and doubts: Christ was with him. And as we have already seen, the same happened again very near the end of Paul's life, when he was on trial. At that point of great vulnerability, when he felt deserted by his friends, he writes that 'the Lord stood at my side and gave me strength' (2 Timothy 4:17).

The compensator for our losses

More than once, and in very strong terms, Jesus warns his followers that being a disciple could be a costly business. But at the same time he promises them rich compensation. Listen, for example, to this: ' "I tell you the truth," Jesus said to them, "no-one who has left home or wife or brothers or parents or children for the sake of the kingdom of God will fail to receive many times as much in this age and, in the age to come, eternal life" ' (Luke 18:29,30).

Could that really be true? Does it sound a bit glib? He is talking about serious losses – home, wife, children... And his hearers knew that the possible losses were real. This was no airy-fairy stuff. How can we understand his promises, then? It's clear that the 'many times as much' compensation isn't literal.

> **His hearers knew that the possible losses were real.**

But can it be real? And in this life as well as the next? Yes, it can!

In the opening chapter of this book, I said I wanted to maintain the right balance between presenting the reality of hardships on the one hand, and the rich compensations on the other. In talking about these things with many people, two conversations stand out. Both were with experienced missionaries who had suffered real hardships. Both of them urged me not to overlook the compensations! That simply confirms the impression I have gained through friendships with many missionaries: they are generally a positive, happy group of people! They have found Christ to be a loving and generous taskmaster. He is a rich compensator.

Counting the cost

If I accept his high call, with its costs, might the 'bottom line' end up 'in the red', with a cost that outweighs the benefits? Never! 'God is no-one's debtor.' That bottom line will always be in the black.

Turn again with me to the New Testament, to Luke 14:25–33. Jesus is telling his hearers that serving him must overshadow all other commitments. He introduces two parables, both of which teach the folly of making an important decision without weighing up the pros and cons. Of course, he has in mind our decision to follow him. He doesn't want followers who rush unthinkingly into discipleship. In one story, he talks of starting a building project without calculating the costs properly; in the other he uses the illustration of a king going to war without assessing his own forces, and those of the enemy.

> **He doesn't want followers who rush unthinkingly into discipleship.**

Do Jesus' stories imply that someone might quite reasonably come to a different conclusion? Is it conceivable that following him might not be worth the cost? No way! If we do the sums right, there is never any doubt about the bottom line.

Jesus is calling us to full-blooded discipleship. Are you ready for that? Would you really settle for anything less?

INTERLUDE

Seven three-minute reads on
issues related to the themes of
this book

Our missionary trinity

John Stott, author, Christian statesman, and IFES Ambassador-at-Large, explains why world mission is at the heart of the gospel.

The whole concept of mission is out of favour with today's pluralistic world, and hostility to it is growing. So it seems to me vital for us to have a sound basis for our involvement in the world mission of the church, and especially important to remember that Christian mission is rooted in the nature of God himself. The Bible reveals him as a missionary God – Father, Son and Holy Spirit – who has a missionary vision, creates a missionary church, and sends it out on a missionary expedition throughout the world.

So, *first*, the God of the Old Testament is a missionary God. God called Abraham some four thousand years ago and promised not only to bless him and his family, but through his posterity to bless all the families of the earth. It is no exaggeration to say that Genesis 12:1–4 is the most unifying text in the Bible. God's whole purpose is encapsulated in it, namely to bless the nations through Christ, who is the seed of Abraham.

Secondly, the Christ of the gospels is a missionary

Christ. True, on two occasions Jesus said that he had been sent only to the lost sheep of the house of Israel, but this was a temporary historical limitation; it related only to his earthly ministry. After his death and his resurrection he commissioned his followers to go to all nations with the 'Good News' and make them his disciples.

Thirdly, the Holy Spirit of the Book of Acts is a missionary Spirit. Pentecost was essentially a missionary event. But Jesus promised that after the Holy Spirit had come upon them, his followers would be his witnesses in Jerusalem, Judea and Samaria, and unto the uttermost parts of the earth. The Book of Acts, in fact, is the fulfilment of that beginning. We watch enthralled as the missionary Spirit creates a missionary people and sends them out on their missionary adventure, beginning in Jerusalem, the capital of Jewry, and ending in Rome, the capital of the world.

How then shall we respond to these things? Have we resisted the missionary dimension of the Church's life? Have we perhaps patronised it rather reluctantly with a few formal prayers and a few grudging coins? If so, we need to repent, that is to change our mind.

You tell me you believe in God. He is a missionary God.

Are you committed to Christ? He is a missionary Christ.

You claim to be filled with the Holy Spirit. He is a missionary Spirit.

It is impossible to avoid these things. Mission is integral to authentic Christianity; Christianity without mission is Christianity no longer. For mission is rooted in the very nature of God himself, Father, Son and Holy Spirit.

UCCF, the IFES movement in the UK, has made this audio-track from John Stott available to download for your church or for use in training events. Go to www.uccf.org.uk/omt

Ten ways to build your world vision

Paul Borthwick serves with Development Associates International, developing leaders in the under-resourced world. He teaches missions at Gordon College and is an Urbana Missions Associate with InterVarsity/USA.

The Bible. This is the starting point. God's plan from Genesis to Revelation, from creation to the end of human history, has been to have fellowship with us. And for the sake of that he gave his one and only Son. As we read the Scriptures the Holy Spirit expands our view of God, of the world, of ourselves. Don't neglect this.

Current events. If we come to the news as God's people, then daily papers and news websites become God's prayer list. World leaders become the subjects of our prayers. Now we are starting to see the world as God sees it.

Prayer. We come to God in prayer because the task is simply too overwhelming for us. When we pray, two things happen. *First*, we remember that God himself is in charge, and the only one who can do this. *Secondly*, we

141

are changed. God sometimes uses our prayers to make us softer and more willing to say, 'Yes, I'll help be the answer to that prayer.' I encourage every Christian to choose a country to be praying for, or a world leader, or a missionary. Be specific as you pray for God's work around the world.

Reading. William Carey caught his interest in God's world not by reading the Bible, but by reading the adventures of Captain Cook in the South Pacific. Reading can build our mission zeal, and our world vision. This can happen through *National Geographic*, news magazines, travel books or biographies.

First-hand experience. It was first-hand experience with the Gentiles that made Peter say, 'I now realise how true it is that God does not show favouritism but accepts men from every nation who fear him and do what is right' (Acts 10:34,35). Serve on a short-term programme, travel across cultures, eat the food of other cultures, go to a worship service in another language. God is not the God just of my people, or of my culture or of my language; our God is the God of the nations.

Friends. The writer to the Hebrews instructs us to 'encourage one another daily... so that none of you may be hardened by sin's deceitfulness' (Hebrews 3:13). Choose to spend time with people who are like-minded, who will encourage you in your praying, who will stimulate you by their reading and conversation, and their own desire to grow spiritually.

Generosity in giving. Money is not a substitute for personal involvement. But it's one way in which we are rich, and by world standards, all of us in the West are rich. We can use our money to invest in the ministry of the gospel. Giving should also include our time.

Meet cross-cultural workers. Get to know them personally as real people, so that your prayer for them can be intelligent. Make the most of chances to meet people who work all over the world: with tribes, in cities, those in the midst of great spiritual revivals, those persevering in difficult places. These conversations can be powerful in building our faith. And they serve to encourage us that we are part of God's team around the world.

Lifestyle choices. Someone once said, 'I've chosen to live more simply that others may simply live.' Lifestyle choice means being willing to cut back on ownership of possessions, and instead free ourselves up so we can give to others. Lifestyle choice might mean getting rid of clothes or cutting back on our food diet. These can be courageous choices in this generation.

Maps and pictures. Have maps on your walls, or pictures of other peoples. This reminds us to pray. Make the map work for you. Mark on it the places where you have friends or missionaries from your church. Mark the countries where you are praying for political leaders.

Many mission agencies run short-term programmes which are put together to include 'hands-on' ministry (so far as language will allow) as well as training. This is a very valuable way to gain exposure to the church in another country, and to roles in which you could serve. YWAM and OM both include residential training for short-termers, from a few weeks up to six months. You will find details on their websites. All programmes have an element of training on the job, as well as advice on good reading and preparation in other ways.

Johnny and Ann McClean work with OMF in Central Thailand, where 95% of the people are Buddhist. They have received many short-termers over the years, and view them from the start as fellow workers.

Ann gives us a glimpse into the short termers' experiences:

Thailand is completely open to the gospel. The government issues missionary visas so we are free to preach and teach. That freedom is what surprises most of our short-term workers. We can preach in the open-air, hold evangelistic

Bible studies with students who had never seen a Bible before, give out tracts, interview Buddhists.

Short-term workers come here from all over the world. For some their time with us is stretching and difficult. But as we start to work together, and share the gospel with the Thai around us, all our short-termers have a sense of awe and privilege. They become part of our ministry, building friendships with people, increasing the Christian presence in the area, helping us to find those who are genuinely interested in knowing more about the gospel. We love it when we see short-termers arriving who are evidently willing to listen, to learn and to grow.

They do all sorts of things. They paint walls, teach English, organise parties and day trips, get involved in the local student fellowship on campus, help with open-air evangelism. Language has its limitations but loving concern and a willingness to show a genuine interest in others goes a long way in building bridges. Many new believers here trace their first contact with Christians to a short-termer who took time to talk, to offer friendship, and to share the most important message in the world.

Very few short-termers see the impact they have, as it can take many more months of Bible study and friendship before a Thai Buddhist comes to faith in Christ.

Only one life

'Helen' has a degree in Geography from Oxford University. We talked with her shortly before she left the UK to live in a country which is a one-party state, and hostile to Christianity. We asked her to tell her story.

I grew up in a supportive and loving family as the eldest of three girls. We were given a good education and my childhood was really happy. My parents worked abroad before we were born. So we grew up with an interest in other cultures, especially the developing world.

I was deeply challenged when I became a Christian as a student. I heard a talk on how God called people to himself from all parts of the world and I began to see that the real problems aren't just poverty, war, and injustice, terrible as these are. But beyond these, we all need to have a restored relationship with God.

I prayed that if God wanted me to take the gospel to people with little opportunity to hear it, I would be willing to go. Having prayed that, my interest in missions just grew. I read books on mission. I visited East Africa and

East Asia, and saw what it's like to live and work there. I prayed, wrote letters to missionaries, and so on.

Up to then I had admired missionaries, but they were really just the stuff of books. Now some had become close friends – just ordinary people who'd said 'Yes' to God's call.

Short-term trips are good for personal growth. Go on one if you have the chance. But we need long-term commitment to the people, to learn the local language, and to adapt to another culture. As I started to think about my own future, I began to ask myself: how do I want to look back on my life? How will I account for how I've used it when I retire, or indeed when Jesus returns?

It hasn't been easy. My friends were finding well-paid, fulfilling jobs, and that was hard. People questioned my right to share my faith with those from a non-Christian culture. Even some of my Christian friends didn't understand what I was doing. But the hardest thing has been to see my parents having to let go some of their hopes for my future. They're concerned about my long-term financial stability, and about limited job prospects back in the UK. They're worried about the reduced likelihood of marriage. And they fear for my health and safety. I've always been very close to my family. And I'm dreading saying 'goodbye' at the airport.

So what's kept me going? I have difficult days, but I'm sure that this is what God wants me to do with my life. Many people are praying for me, even some I hardly know, which is amazing. Finance has come in, and I've been stunned by the love and support of my church. It's been great to see how God has used my situation to challenge others about mission.

Life won't be easy. I'm going to an area where the Church is persecuted, where my mail and my e-mails are likely to be read, and possibly my phone tapped. And it's a difficult and dangerous place to live in. But I keep on reminding myself of Jesus' words in Mark 8:34–36:

> *If anyone would come after me, he must deny himself and take up his cross and follow me. For whoever wants to save his life will lose it, but whoever loses his life for me and for the gospel will save it. What good is it for a man to gain the whole world, yet forfeit his soul?*

And then there are the words from Romans 10:14:

> *How can they believe in the one of whom they have not heard? And how can they hear without someone preaching to them?*

I have only one life and I want to grasp that one chance to live wholeheartedly for God.

Africa's needs

We asked Joshua Wathanga from Kenya for his views on the African church and its needs. Joshua trained as a vet in Scotland and served with Kenya FOCUS and then with the International Fellowship of Evangelical Students.

Does Africa still need western missionaries?

So long as the Great Commission has not been completed, the answer has to be yes. We still need people to cross cultures but it is no longer one-way traffic. There will be non-westerners whom God will call to the West to be a witness to his saving grace. So the question is not whether Africa needs cross-cultural workers, but what kind of people it needs. This new breed of missionary will, like those who have gone before, be motivated by a love for Christ, and will have a love for Africa too. This is not a glib thing to say, because Africa is not getting easier to work in. It is ravaged by poverty, war and disease. It is being strangulated by political misgovernance. It is bleeding from corruption. It is suffering from violence and carelessness in the society as a result. So going to Africa is not a great adventure or a picture safari. It will be very hard work and can be very dangerous.

Tell us more about the type of person that is needed
They would not be locked up in a missionary compound hoping to make an occasional evangelistic raid into the natives' territory. We need men and women ready to roll up their sleeves and work alongside Africans in making disciples in a very difficult context. This new breed of missionary has to be sensitive to the fact that not all western contributions have been helpful. Some have been harmful, but to have a western background and history need not minimise effectiveness, as missionaries are there not as westerners but as obedient servants of the Lord Jesus Christ.

What advice would you give to new missionaries?
They should be aware of a certain reality in most of Africa – a lack of confidence, not least due to the history of colonialism. Most Africans need to be helped to some empowerment. Missionaries should go prepared to train up and mentor African leaders who will in time replace them. This will encourage people to take responsibility for God's call upon their lives. And finally, this new breed of missionary will go prepared to learn and be changed, whilst working with Africans as equals, so exercising true partnership in the gospel.

How do you see this in relation to the Church?
Most new missionaries are surprised to find a vibrant church making serious inroads as salt and light into society, and a Church which is strong both numerically and in evangelistic fervour. To be sure, it is a relatively

young church, with many needs – discipleship, theological training, good Christian literature, student ministry, to name just a few.

Let me close by saying missionaries to Africa are likely to find themselves challenged about their own love for Christ and their understanding of the cost of discipleship as they observe God at work in what used to be called a dark continent.

Thank you, Joshua

Sending people into tough situations

The author explains how mission agencies can send people to face tough situations. He has children of his own. How does he feel about sending people like that to face difficulties?

I think we should feel sensitive to sending people out into hard situations, and we do. There are some areas we wouldn't expose people to, depending on their age and experience. I think for example of places where there is a high level of violence, or extreme isolation. There again, that depends on the person's resilience.

But I don't think we should feel uneasy or ashamed about encouraging people to think about the possibility of places where the going will be tough.

I say that for two reasons. First, those who work in the sending offices of missions should themselves be willing to go where God sends them and I trust they are willing. Many have long experience of serving overseas, some in affluent cultures like Japan or Europe, or parts of the Middle East; others in the two-thirds world, with the poverty and lack of facilities we find there. They have already made those difficult decisions we talk about in this book. They know how hard it can be. So we're calling people to go down a path we have already trodden, or I hope are willing to tread.

And yes, I have to face that hard question as a parent too, should God call my children down that path.

My second answer touches on something more important. It is the issue of authority. We're not taking it on ourselves to direct other people's lives, to impose our wills on theirs, to tell them what to do. We're encouraging people to discern whether God is calling them to go, and that difference is crucial. And if we or they think such a path is right for them, we will encourage them to recognise God's authority and to obey.

But it's an authority issue for us too. Those serving in mission agencies believe God is still calling people to go abroad worldwide. They're going in their thousands, and they're needed. Spreading the gospel is not a finished task. So the church and mission agencies need to be active in teaching and in encouraging people to think about these things. When we do that, we're not imposing our own wills on others, we're simply obeying God.

Discovering God's will is a joint process. Part of the process is intensely personal of course, as we each work out the implications of discipleship in our own relationship with God. But our self-understanding is fallen. We need the help of others. Our church leaders and older friends often have a better insight than we do into our gifts and abilities. We need to hear them. If we're going to work in a missionary society or as part of another kind of team, then the leaders will play a key role in discerning what openings will match our gifts. These are all ways in which God directs us, and we shouldn't ignore them.

Maybe I can say to those who have got this far with the book, if you're at the stage of needing to clarify your way ahead, do talk with older Christians. May God bless you richly as you explore his good plan for you.

Getting ready to go

- **Prepare yourself.** You are carrying a message of life and death. The way you live will display the gospel, or dishonour it.

- **Ask friends to pray.** Invite a few friends to pray for you regularly, and give them good information on your prayer needs.

- **Learn about your host country:** its Church, people, culture, customs. If you know any nationals living or studying in your country, ask to see their photographs; talk about their families. Find out about the politics, and about how religious beliefs influence the culture and practices of everyday life.

- **Follow current events.** If you are familiar with the language, reading the national newspapers of your host country on the web will be instructive. If not, read the local English-language papers which you could find through a search engine. This will give you news and comment from within the country.

- **Be prepared for difficulties.** Relationships can be a source of stress, especially if there is conflict with fellow Christians. (See Chapter 3)

- **Go with a servant heart.** We represent the Christ who came to serve. We will find much to learn from our host culture which enriches us personally, and enriches the way we express the gospel to others.

PART II

GOD'S MISSIONARY HEART: FROM EDEN TO ETERNITY

About the author

Rose Dowsett serves with OMF International in its conference and training ministry. She became a Christian shortly before starting at Bristol University in the UK, where she and others prayed regularly for world mission. Their particular prayer was for Christ's name to be honoured in the world's universities. Rose met her husband Dick while serving on the staff of the British IFES movement, UCCF. They then joined OMF International, and were seconded for eight years to the staff of the Philippines IFES movement, the InterVarsity Christian Fellowship. Rose is Vice-chairman of the World Evangelical Alliance Mission Commission and chairs the Interserve International Council. She is author of *The Great Commission* (OMF/Monarch). The Dowsetts live in Glasgow, Scotland, and have three grown-up children.

God's missionary heart: from Eden to eternity

In the beginning, God

*B*efore time and space began, God existed, eternally. There has never been a moment, a dimension or a planet when he hasn't been there. When time and this earth as we know it come to an end, he will still be there – at the heart of the new creation. Between Genesis and Revelation lie thousands of years of human history. The Bible record tells the story from the beginning of the world to the end of the first century AD. From then until now the story is continued through the life of the Church.

In Genesis 1 and 2, we read that human beings, uniquely among all creation, were made by God 'in his image', reflecting in a special way what God is like. We were made to be God's friends, to walk and talk with him, to enjoy love and communication and mutual delight, and to care for his creation.

A plan ruined?

When the first man and woman tried to make themselves equal with God, to be the original rather than the image, that was a tragedy beyond imagination for the whole human race, and as decisive a point in history as the creation itself had been. On the one hand, God's love and desire to enjoy their fellowship remained unchanged. On the other, human disobedience had distorted the 'imageness', had shattered the reflective mirror, and made people by instinct fugitives from God rather than happy subjects under his kingship. This disobedience – sin – meant banishment from the intimate

> **Anger and sorrow mixed in God.**

friendship with God for which we were created; as a result anger and sorrow mixed in God.

Our missionary God

If that were the end of the story, it would be bleak despair indeed. Perhaps you wonder why, in a book such as this, we start here. The answer is simple. The whole of the rest of human history is the story of God's commitment to effect reconciliation; to welcome men and women back into friendship with him; to deal with sin at its root. The whole of the Bible story, from Genesis to Revelation, pulses with his longing for people to turn back to him; and in every generation the task of bringing that message to the nations is as urgent as it has ever been.

If we miss this when we read the Bible, we miss the point completely. As John Stott makes clear (page 139), mission is rooted in the character of God, not an optional extra we can take or leave, something for a handful of Christians to get involved in. To ignore the imperative to be mission-breathing, mission-living people shows a total misreading of both the Old and New Testaments. We simply can't be authentic Bible-believing Christians and not be missionary Christians. We can't be an authentic

> **Mission is no divine afterthought.**

church and not be a missionary church. For our triune God – Father, Son and Holy Spirit – is most profoundly a missionary God; and we who are made in his image are called to reflect his nature, his truth, his heart concerns. Mission is no divine afterthought. It's integral to everything.

Heaven by way of the cross

The book of Revelation is difficult to understand, and has often given rise to passionate arguments among Christians over how to interpret it. But the Holy Spirit, who inspired the writer, John, gave us this part of the Bible because we need it. It provides a glimpse of God's eternal goal: people from every language and ethnic group, down through the centuries and right around the world, worshipping him face to face, enjoying the fellowship with him for which we were created and are being recreated. Here is the Kingdom of God lived out in its radiance and fulfilment.

If that is God's goal for us and for the world, it needs to fill our horizons, for it is wonderful beyond our imagining, and far beyond our present experience. To achieve that goal, God graciously invites us to be his fellow workers. What higher privilege can there be than to work with him in bringing his gospel of reconciliation to this world?

> **There could be no joy in heaven were it not for the death of our Lord Jesus.**

At the very centre of the new heaven and new earth is the Lamb, who carries the marks of Calvary. Here we have the vivid and inescapable reminder that there could be no joy in

165

heaven were it not for the death of our Lord Jesus, in our place, on our behalf, and to bear our sin. The life, death, resurrection and ascension of the Lord Jesus mark the central point of all history, spanning back as far as the creation, and forwards to the end of time. The cross is not a stirring example of courageous self-sacrifice by a brave man; it is the unique and decisive event by which God himself, in the person of the Son, dealt once and for all with the problem of sin and fallenness. Everything before it led up to that point; everything since looks back to it, as well as forward to the end of time.

Made in the image of the Trinity

We can understand our true identity and significance only when we see our 'now' in the context of this great story – this divine metanarrative – arching from the beginning of time to its end. All three persons of the Trinity are fully involved. God the Father so loved the world that he gave his only Son. God the Son so loved the world that he left his rightful place in all the glory of heaven to stand in our place through birth, life, death and resurrection, to deal with sin and the rift it had caused between us and the God to whom we belong. Father and Son together so loved us that they sent the Holy Spirit, God making his home within and among those who have come alive through faith in the Lord Jesus.

Our triune God – Father, Son and Holy Spirit – is Creator, Sustainer, Life-giver, Redeemer, Judge and King. He is Emmanuel: 'God with us'. In all these aspects of his being we see a single golden thread: God reaching out to his creatures in love and mercy, in righteousness and holiness. We

> **We are created in his image, *Imago Dei*, to be like him.**

are created in his image, *Imago Dei*, to be like him, and in the whole of our lives, through word, deed and character, to bear witness to his missionary heart.

Reading the Old Testament in the light of Christ

Shortly after his resurrection and before his ascension, the Lord Jesus appeared, unrecognised, to two sorrowing disciples, as they walked from Jerusalem to the village of Emmaus. They were evidently deep in conversation, and he asked them what they were talking about. They explained how women had gone to the tomb and found it empty, and how these women heard from the angels that Jesus had risen from the dead and was alive again. But despite this, they remained confused and downcast. So 'beginning with Moses and all the Prophets, he explained to them what was said in all the Scriptures concerning himself' (Luke 24:27). Only later as they ate together did these two men recognise Jesus.

> **They remained confused and downcast.**

Let's not miss what is happening here. Jesus is saying that he is the grid through which we understand the Old Testament, the lens through which we must read it. And indeed we see in the Acts sermons, and in the letters to the young churches, that the apostles and early disciples taught the Old Testament in this way, reinterpreting its story through that grid, through that lens, in the light of what they now knew about Jesus Christ.

Stephen's address to the Sanhedrin is a good example of this. His life was already in danger and he was fully aware that the Jewish authorities would be inflamed to hear him interpret their scriptures as referring to Jesus. But

167

he feels he has no choice, and Acts 7 records his courageous declaration in detail.

He traces salvation history from Abraham right through the law and the prophets and on to the crucifixion. Stephen sees so clearly how that 'golden thread' of God's mission has gleamed right down the centuries. As he then goes on to urge the Sanhedrin to realise that the prophets had been sent for their sakes, and that they are resisting the Holy Spirit, they are enraged. At this point the Holy Spirit gives him a special glimpse of heaven, that final goal. 'Look,' he said, 'I see heaven open and the Son of Man standing at the right hand of God' (Acts 7:56). With that he is dragged off to be stoned, with Saul (later to become the apostle Paul) looking on.

Once, then, the disciples grasped this golden thread, it became an urgent priority for them – to demonstrate in their evangelism, and to teach to the Church.

Tracing the story back to its beginning

The story of mission begins in Genesis 3, when Adam and Eve rebelled against God, breaking the fellowship they had with him. It is only when we grasp the importance of this chapter that we can understand Paul's tight reasoning in Romans 5, or his reference to Christ as the last Adam (1 Corinthians 15:45). From that very point of rebellion in our human history we needed a Redeemer who could make atonement for sins, who could restore that fellowship, for we were unable to do it ourselves. That Redeemer could only be the eternal and sinless Son of God, born as a Man and dying in our place. We can trace the genealogy of the Lord Jesus Christ right back to Adam.

Noah's ark has often been reduced to a sentimental domesticated zoo.

Nine generations down from Adam we have Noah. The story of Noah's ark (Genesis 6) is a terrible one. We frequently miss that, because it has often been reduced to a sentimental domesticated zoo for children, or even a children's cartoon.

> *The LORD saw how great*
> *man's wickedness on the*
> *earth had become, and that*
> *every inclination of the*
> *thoughts of his heart was*
> *only evil all the time. The*
> *LORD was grieved that he*
> *had made man on the earth,*
> *and his heart was filled with*
> *pain.* (Genesis 6:5,6)

Here we read of the appalling spiral of human wickedness as people lived out anarchic independence from God; this was followed by such devastating divine judgement that only Noah and his family – a total of eight people – survived.

Before the flood came, God warned Noah, and told him to build the ark that was to be his means of escape. We can imagine the jeers of neighbours, as this was long before the first drop of rain fell, but Noah doggedly obeyed in faith. God had said, 'This is how you will be saved' – and Noah believed him, obeyed him, and was indeed saved.

Ten generations further on we meet Abram, later to become Abraham, the first-recorded cross-cultural missionary. He was born in Ur of the Chaldeans and his family later settled in Haran. Genesis 12 records the story of God's call to him to set out from Haran on a journey of faith to an unknown destination.

Embedded in the call, and in its accompanying promise of great future blessing, is the purpose for which it was designed: 'all peoples on earth will be blessed through you' (Genesis 12:3). In due time, Abraham became the founding father of that great people, the Jews, the children of Israel. God called them 'my people' not because they were better than everybody else, nor because they were the only ones God was interested in, but because they were to be the real-life arena in which he could show what he was like, communicate his word and demonstrate his deeds. God's people were to be a visual aid, a three-dimensional, living, breathing demonstration of who God is, what he demands, and what it means to know him – so that the surrounding nations, looking on, could say 'Ah! So that's what the true and living God is like! That is who he is! Let's worship him and follow him, too.'

So right from the start God's people were called to declare and show the truth about the one true and living God, so that the nations, deluded by false religions and tribal gods, could hear and see, repent and believe and obey. This was no disembodied philosophy, but the incarnation (albeit rather shadowy) of God's word and character in individuals and communities. Yes, the mirror might be rather dim, but through them God would be recognisably God in terms people could understand and relate to.

God's missionary heart for all nations

As we travel on through the Old Testament – its poetry and narrative, instruction, prophecy and miraculous events, we see how God reveals more and more about himself. Over and over again he reaches out, takes the initiative, displays his missionary heart for all nations, not just for the Israelites. It is amazing to see how often 'foreigners' are drawn to faith in the living God through divine initiative. Here are just a few examples.

Take Rahab, whose family were the sole survivors of the destruction of Jericho (Joshua chapters 2,6), who went on to become an ancestress of great King David, and who appears both in the genealogy of Christ (Matthew 1:5), and in the remarkable portrait gallery of people of faith (Hebrews 11:31).

Or take Ruth, a defenceless widow of the discredited Moabites, who comes to faith in the true God through the testimony of Naomi, her mother-in-law. Ruth then also becomes an ancestress of David and, centuries later, of the Lord Jesus.

Think of arrogant King Nebuchadnezzar of Babylon, to whom God sends Daniel and his friends, through the painful experience of capture and exile. Their faithful witness, by word and life, and God's miraculous deliverance, leads this most implacable enemy of God to be humbled into submission, worship and testimony. (Trace the story in Daniel 1-4.)

God sends Elijah to a widow in Sidon, to save her from starvation and death, and to draw her to faith (1 Kings 17:7–24). He sends Jonah, rebellious and reluctant though he may be, to Nineveh, with the result that tens of thousands repent and believe. The Israelites hated the Ninevites, but God loved them.

He sends an enslaved Israelite servant girl and the prophet Elisha to cure a Syrian general of leprosy, and to bring him to faith (2 Kings 5).

God's yearning for those outside Israel is emphasised in the teaching of the prophets, and in the poetry of the psalms. Repeatedly we read statements such as:

The Lord is the great God,
the great King above all
gods. (Psalm 95:3)

Sing to the Lord ... Declare
his glory among the
nations... all the gods of the
nations are idols, but the
Lord made the heavens... He
will judge the world in
righteousness... (Psalm 96)

And foreigners who bind
themselves to the Lord to
serve him, to love the name
of the Lord, and to worship
him... who hold fast to my
covenant – these I will bring
to my holy mountain and
give them joy in my house of
prayer. (Isaiah 56:6–7)

> **The gospels**
> **demonstrate**
> **just how**
> **subversive**
> **Christ's life and**
> **ministry was.**

The gospels are full of incidents and teaching which demonstrate just how subversive Christ's life and ministry was in the face of the Jews' racism, and of their certainty that they were automatically protected by God. The prologue to the whole New Testament, the opening chapter of Matthew's Gospel, explosively sets both foreigners and women at the heart of Jesus' ancestral line. The next chapter opens with foreigners – the Magi, astrologers from the East – being led by the Spirit of God through revelation and dreams to worship the child born King. On page after page of the Gospels we find men, women and children who for one reason or another would be regarded as outside God's saving purpose, to whom Jesus comes with the word of life and salvation.

The consistent pattern is of God's love reaching out far beyond the boundaries of the people of Israel; the God of Israel is no tribal God, but the one and only true God of the whole universe.

God reaches out, but his people turn away

Over and over again we see God making an overture towards the people of Israel, whose dismal habit was to turn away from him. The prophecy of Hosea (8th century BC) is one of the most poignant sections of the Old Testament, as God pours out his pain and heartache using the picture of an unfaithful bride. Even against this appalling picture of sin and rebellion, comes the plea to God's people to return in repentance so that they may be forgiven and restored.

Not only did the Israelites often turn their backs on God, but they regarded themselves as the only intended recipients of his care. Such self-centredness is hard to grasp – were it not for the sobering fact that the Church has often behaved in the same way: 'God's blessing is for us, and let's ignore the rest of the world.' By the time of Christ, far from understanding their privilege and responsibility to reach out to surrounding nations to bring them salvation, most Jews had wrongly interpreted the prophecies of the Messiah, and turned him into a political deliverer who would free Israel from occupying forces and destroy all but themselves. Love and protection for the alien, as instructed by God (e.g. Leviticus 24:22; Exodus 23:9), had become hostility.

This is one of the reasons why so few people could recognise Jesus' identity as the Messiah: they were looking for the wrong sort of person. And it is also why the people in the synagogue at Nazareth, initially praising him, so soon turned violently against him and tried to kill him: he insisted that God's love reached beyond themselves, and illustrated this by reminding them that Elijah was led to an alien widow, not an Israelite, and Naaman the Syrian was healed of leprosy whereas there were still lepers in Israel (Luke 4:14–30).

The cross and resurrection

It is supremely in the cross and resurrection that we see God's missionary heartbeat. Had Jesus been only an inspired teacher, a loving example, a good man, we could be inspired and challenged but we could not be set right with God as we needed to be. Paul tells us that 'when the time had fully come, God sent his Son, born of a woman, born under law, to redeem those under law, that we might receive the full rights of sons. Because you are sons, God sent the Spirit of his Son into our hearts, the Spirit who calls out "Abba, Father" ' (Galatians 4:4–6). Here is God taking the initiative, reaching out, sending his Son and his Spirit. Why? Because he longs to restore us to a perfect father-child relationship with himself.

And so the Lord Jesus, in fulfilment of Old Testament prophecy (e.g. Isaiah 53:10), was crushed and broken on the cross; he identified totally with sin and sinner in order to deal decisively and finally with sin and its fallout (Romans 16:20, Hebrews 2:13–15, Revelation 12:9; 20:2, etc.). Taking place at a particular point in time and geography, this once-for-all momentous event was already known in the courts of eternity; so Hebrews 11 can declare that those who responded in repentance, faith and obedience to God's overtures in Old Testament days, long before Christ died and rose again in time – these, too, entered into the eternal Kingdom. The resurrection is God's triumphant 'It is done!' to dealing with sin and death and alienation.

And so the Lord Jesus, walking that afternoon along the road to Emmaus, could unpack the Old Testament Scriptures, and show how event after event illustrated the missionary God at work, and prophecy after prophecy pointed to the Son who would come and turn promise into completed achievement.

And the work achieved by the Son was not only for that generation, or for the Jewish people, but for all time, all generations, all people groups of the world. That is why the gospel is not just 'good news' but the very best of all good news ever. And that is why all the world needs to hear it and see it, and to have an opportunity to respond.

The Bible is not a random rag-bag of stories, of times and places long ago and far away. No, says Jesus, there is a continuous golden thread running all the way through, even through the puzzling bits: God who made us and the whole world is the same God who sustains us, and keeps everything going. Ever since the Garden of Eden and that first question, 'Where are you?' (Genesis 3:9), he has been searching for the lost, because he wants us to be found.

> **The Bible is not a random rag-bag of stories.**

The Spirit and the Church

The resurrection is not the last word either. It is followed by the ascension, and that continuous ever-present ministry of Christ as he 'always lives to intercede' for those whom he saves (Hebrews 7:25). Here is God our advocate in heaven! What stronger appeal could there be than his?

The Lord Jesus promised that after he left his disciples, they would not have long to wait before the Holy Spirit would come to make his home within and among them. And that is exactly what took place at Pentecost, as Luke records for us in Acts 2. Notice what happened. The Spirit is not given primarily so that the disciples could have amazing experiences. We see this from the start. The first thing that happens is that the Spirit enables them to communicate in many languages to the people from all over the world gathered in Jerusalem to celebrate the festival of Passover: everyone hears the story of Jesus in their own native language. The Holy Spirit, equally with Father and Son, is a missionary Spirit.

The early church quickly realised that they must look to the Spirit to lead them wherever he wanted to take them. Wherever they went, as they went, they were to make disciples. They were to explain the good news in words by preaching and teaching, by debating, by chatting, by writing. They were to demonstrate the good news by transformed personal lives, and by transformed communities. They were to point to heaven but live robustly on earth. They were to expect signs and wonders, healings and miracles, where God sovereignly chose to give them, yet live in faith and faithfulness in the ordinariness of the everyday. In such

> They were to point to heaven but live robustly on earth.

ways the Kingdom of God would become visible, and people come to know the King. And ever since, the Church has always been truest to herself when she has given herself in obedience to this heavenly vision.

And so we come full circle back to God's call to Abram. God's people were to be a missionary people, for the blessing of the nations, enabling everyone in the world to learn the truth about the one and only living God. In establishing the church as the people of God, that purpose was renewed: to disciple the nations, so that men and women of every people group, all ages and each generation, might come to worship God and one day be part of that triumphant community in heaven.

And this is where you come in. For you, too, are made in the image of God, and are called to reflect his missionary heart, his missionary deeds, his missionary words. Some of us will do this in our own nation, among our own ethnic group and the diversity of peoples now living in our home country. Some of us will be called to serve in other nations. Wherever we serve, our calling is the same.

> **Wherever we serve, our calling is the same.**

Jesus says 'Go!' and as you go, make disciples.

This goes to George Verwer of Operation Mobilisation.

'Don't waste your life'

God has put it on my heart to say that this is a great book. But I hope we won't be satisfied in just reading it, and getting a blessing or saying, 'Yes, this is good!' or 'Yes, this needs to be said!' or 'Oh yes, my friend really needs to pay attention to this.' We must all now take some practical steps in our own lives to be more Christ-like, more focused, more biblical disciples. Let's ask for God's grace to be marathon-runners for him as a result of this.

I was asked recently what I look for in new workers. We need people who are willing to learn, especially since the first one or two years is training. Many short-termers then realise they are not cross-cultural missionaries, and they return home to be effective, we trust, in their own culture. I believe the bottom line for new workers in all cases is knowing Christ personally and having a dynamic walk with him, and then being ready to learn. I look for grace, discipline, the crucified life, the Spirit-filled life, flexibility, big-heartedness and other Christ-like attributes. Of course to some degree you have to learn these along the way.

Be willing to show this book to others in your church. We need more people to be mission-mobilisers, to talk about world mission, because a lot of Christians have very little understanding of what God is doing, of the opportunities there are, and of the phenomenal fulfilment and privilege we have in this kind of work.

God is calling us all to be a part of His mission. Don't waste your life.

George Verwer

Mission Agencies

Some agencies work in one geographic region, or with particular people groups. Others work globally. This book is published by OMF International, SIM and IFES.

OMF works in East Asia and among East Asian peoples around the world; SIM in Africa, South America and Asia. Their ministries are varied: evangelism and church planting, teaching, literature work, medical work and placing Christians with professional skills, especially where the majority religion is hostile to the Christian faith.

IFES is working to proclaim Christ in the world's universities. It is a fellowship of national student movements in over 150 countries. These movements carry a range of names. Many English-speaking movements are known as FES; others as UCCF (UK); InterVarsity (US, Canada); TSCF (NZ). They equip students to be (i) effective evangelists; (ii) serious disciples; (iii) mission-minded Christians. There are still eighteen countries with no known witness to Christ in their universities.

In common with all evangelical agencies, the central purpose of OMF, SIM and IFES is to bring glory to God through building up his Church. To this end we work in partnership with churches locally and nationally.

Most mission agencies have a regular magazine or webzine. They also send out news and prayer bulletins for friends and supporters who want to get behind the work by praying. If you don't already receive this first-hand news from one or two missions, why not start to?

Don't think of this only in terms of 'being on their database'. It's *much* more. Praying and giving, and encouraging your friends to do the same, is to play a strategic role in the wonderful task of pushing back the frontiers of Christ's kingdom.

For a full list of evangelical missions with a sending base in your country, contact the following:

AUSTRALIA
Mission Interlink
www.evangelicalalliance.org.au

HONG KONG
Hong Kong Association of Christian Missions
www.hkacm.org.hk

MALAYSIA
Malaysian Evangelical Fellowship Missions & Evangelism Commission
PO Box 58, 46700 Petaling Jaya
Tel: 3 735 7328
kohgl@attglobal.net

NETHERLANDS
Eedrachtstraat 29a, 3784 KA Terschuur
Tel: 342 462666
omf_nl@compuserve.com

NEW ZEALAND
Missions Interlink
PO Box 27548, Mt.Roskill, Auckland 1030
Phone: 9 625 0030
missions.jenkins@xtra.co.nz

PHILIPPINES
Philippine Missions Association
PO Box M-006, 1550 Mandaluyong City
Phone: 2 533 6075
pma@jmf.org.ph

SINGAPORE
Singapore Centre for Evangelism & Missions
PO Box 1052, Raffles City, Singapore 9117
Phone: 325 1237
www.scem.info

SOUTH AFRICA
World Mission Centre
PO Box 36147 Menlo Park, 0102
Phone: 12 343 1165
www.worldmissioncentre.com

UK
Global Connections
Whitefield House, 186 Kennington Park Road,
London, SE11 4BT
Phone: 020 7207 2156
www.globalconnections.co.uk

USA

Advancing Churches in Missions Commitment
4201 North Peachtree Road, Suite 300,
Atlanta, GA 30341
Phone: 770 455 8808
www.acmc.org

Evangelical Fellowship of Mission Agencies
4201 North Peachtree Road, Suite 300,
Atlanta, GA 30341
Phone: 770 457 6677
www.efma.gospelcom.net

Interdenominational Foreign Mission Association
PO Box 398, Wheaton, Illinois 60189
Phone: 630 682 9270
www.ifmamissions.org

Bible Colleges

The colleges below offer full-time and part-time training courses for cross-cultural mission or for other kinds of long-term biblical ministry. Some also have distance-learning arrangements. This is not an exhaustive list, and it doesn't imply anything about those not featured. For a full list of residential and non-residential colleges in your country, please consult the agencies in Appendix 1.

Australia
Bible College of Queensland www.bcq.qld.edu.au
Bible College of South Australia
    www.biblecollege.sa.edu.au
Bible College of Victoria www.bcv.vic.edu.au
Moore Theological College www.moore.edu.au
Morling College www.morling.nsw.edu.au
Ridley Theological College www.ridley.unimelb.edu.au
Sydney Missionary and Bible College www.smbc.com.au
Trinity Theological College www.trinity.org.au

Canada
Acadia Divinity College www.adc.acadiau.ca
Atlantic Baptist University www.abu.nb.ca

Briercrest Bible College & Seminary www.briercrest.ca
McMaster University & Divinity School www.macdiv.ca
Providence College www.providence.mb.ca
Regent College, Vancouver www.regent-college.edu
Trinity Western University www.twu.ca
Tyndale Bible College & Seminary
    www.tyndale-canada.edu
Wycliffe College www.wycliffecollege.ca

Malaysia
Malaysia Baptist Theological Seminary www.mbts.net.my

Netherlands
Cornerstone Centre for Intercultural Studies
    www.cornerstone-mtc.com
Evangelische Bijbelscholen
    www.che.nl, www.ebsveenendaal.nl
Azusa Theologische Hogeschool www.azusa.nl
De Wittenberg www.dewittenberg.nl
Free University of Amsterdam (Masters courses)
    www.ph.vu.nl/english

New Zealand
Bible College of New Zealand www.bcnz.ac.nz
Carey Baptist College www.carey.ac.nz
Faith Bible College www.fbc.ac.nz
New Covenant Int'l Bible College www.ncibc.ac.nz
Pathways College of Bible and Mission www.pathways.ac.nz

Singapore
Discipleship Training Centre www.dtc-singapore.org
Singapore Bible College www.sbc.edu.sg
Trinity Theological College www.ttc.edu.sg
Biblical Graduate School of Theology www.bgst.edu.sg

South Africa
Africa School of Mission www.asm.co.za
Baptist Theol College of Southern Africa www.btc.co.za
Bible Institute-Eastern Cape
www.pechurchnet.co.za/bibleinstituteeastcape
Cornerstone Christian College www.cornerstone.org.za
Evangelical Seminary of Southern Africa www.essa.ac.za
South African Theological Seminary www.sats.edu.za
George Whitefield College www.gwc.ac.za

United Kingdom
All Nations Christian College www.allnations.ac.uk
Belfast Bible College www.belfastbiblecollege.com
Cornhill Training Course www.proctrust.org.uk
Evangelical Theol College of Wales www.etcw.ac.uk
International Christian College www.icc.ac.uk
King's Bible College and Training Centre www.kbctc.org
London School of Theology www.lst.ac.uk
Moorlands College www.moorlands.ac.uk
Oak Hill College www.oakhill.ac.uk
Redcliffe College www.redcliffe.org

USA
Columbia International University www.ciu.edu
Fuller Theological Seminary www.fuller.edu
Gordon Conwell Theological Seminary
www.gordonconwell.edu
Moody Bible Institute www.moody.edu
Multnomah Bible College www.multnomah.edu
North Park Theological Seminary www.northpark.edu
Trinity International University www.tiu.edu
Wheaton College www.wheaton.edu

Jesus prayed:

Father, I want those you have given me to be with me where I am, and to see my glory, the glory you have given me because you loved me before the creation of the world. (John 17:24)